108 QUESTIONS CHILDREN ASK ABOUT FRIENDS AND SCHOOL

108

Questions Children Ask about friends& school

Writers:
David R. Veerman, M.Div.
James C. Galvin, Ed.D.
Richard Osborne

Contributors:
J. Alan Sharrer
Ed Strauss

Illustrator:
Lillian Crump

Tyndale House Publishers, Inc. Wheaton, Illinois

Visit Tyndale's exciting Web site at www.tyndale.com

Series designed by Jane Joseph

Produced for Tyndale by Lightwave Publishing and The Livingstone Corporation. David R. Veerman, James C. Galvin, J. Alan Sharrer, Livingstone project staff.

Library of Congress Cataloging-in-Publication Data

Veerman, David.
   108 questions children ask about friends and school / writers, David R. Veerman, James C. Galvin, Richard Osborne ; contributors, J. Alan Sharrer, Ed Strauss ; illustrator, Lillian Crump.
     p. cm.
   ISBN 0-8423-5182-5 (pbk. : alk. paper)
   1. Child rearing—Religious aspects—Christianity—Miscellanea.
2. Children's questions and answers. 3. Friendshp in children—Biblical teaching—Miscellanea. 4. School children—Conduct of life—Biblical teaching—Miscellanea. I. Galvin, James C. II. Osborne, Rick. III. Sharrer, J. Alan. IV. Strauss, Ed. V. Title. VI. Title: One hundred eight questions children ask about friends and school.
BV4526.2.V4   1999
649′.124—dc21   99-12588

CONTENTS

NOTE FROM THE WRITERS

Every person has an inborn need for relationships—the need to love and be loved. It's no wonder, then, that our children want to have enjoyable and affirming friendships. And the older they get, the more important friends become. As a result, our children will naturally ask about how to make friends, how to be a good friend, and how to navigate the sometimes stormy seas of friendship.

As children get involved in school, these questions about friends will increase, as will, quite naturally, the questions about teachers, homework, classes, and the fledgling pressures of academia.

One of those growing pressures is the push for popularity. Actually, this pressure usually results from the issues related to the combination of friends and school. Children want to be accepted and liked, and they enjoy being with the kids who seem to make things happen on campus. Thus, popularity will also engender a multitude of questions, some of them pretty tough.

Easy responses to tough questions are "I don't know!" or "Just because!" or "Because I said so!" These may be responses, but they're not answers. And they certainly don't help the child sort truth from error.

These tough questions are the reason for this book. We collected hundreds of questions children asked about friends and school as well as about the related issue of popularity. Then we identified 108 of the most common and important ones and sorted them into categories. If you are a parent of children ages three to ten or if you work with children, you have surely heard questions like these 108. If not, you soon will.

After identifying Bible passages relevant to each question, we answer the question, summarizing the Bible's application. Study the Scriptures listed, because the Bible has a lot to say about relationships—in the neighborhood and at school. It doesn't answer every question directly, but it gives principles that Christians should know and follow.

As you answer children's questions, keep in mind the following points:

- **"Silly" questions are serious questions.** Always take children's questions seriously. Don't laugh at them. Some questions may sound silly to you, but they're not silly to your child. Be careful not to ridicule your child's imaginative ideas.
- **Some questions reflect a child's immediate personal concerns.** For example, when a little girl asks, "If my friends ignore me, should I ignore them?" (question 33), she's asking about her friends, not just the reaction she should exhibit. She knows that being ignored is not fun and that friends should not ignore other friends. She wants assurance that true friends will not ignore her. Go ahead and answer the "question behind the question": assure your child that true friends do not ignore other friends. If you suspect that there may be a hidden question but don't know what it is, a great way to get at it is to say, "Why do you ask?" or "Why do you want to know?"
- **The best answers come from Scripture.** The Bible doesn't answer every curiosity, but it is the only authoritative source we have for information on how to live in this world. The best thing you can do to prepare to answer questions like these is to study the Scriptures yourself.
- **The best answers avoid theological jargon.** Use normal words. Children think in literal terms, so abstract concepts are meaningless to them. As much as possible, talk about *events* and *objects* that

they can imagine. Describe a smell. Mention a specific thing. Talk about an action, such as running. Give them something to look at in their minds. If they can see it, they will understand it.
- **Some questions have no answer.** Be careful not to make up an answer when you don't have one and when the Bible is silent. If you don't have an answer, say so. Or suggest that you look for the answer together. If you get in the habit of inventing answers, your child will later lump faith with stories and superstitions they've discovered are false. Emphasize the truths of Scripture that you *do* know.
- **Some kids just want to keep asking.** Be ready for follow-up questions and be willing to keep talking. Your answer may lead to more questions. That's the mark of a good answer—it makes the child think.

We wrote this book to help you answer kids' questions about friends, school, and being popular. We sincerely hope and pray it does that.
—Dave Veerman, Jim Galvin, and Rick Osborne

GETTING TO KNOW YOU

Making Friends

Q: HOW DO I MAKE FRIENDS?

A: The first step is to look for places where you might find friends. Actually, potential friends are everywhere—in your neighborhood, at school, on your sports team, and at church. You probably already know a lot of kids who could become very good friends.

The best way to make friends is to be friendly. In other words, you should be the kind of person that others will like to have as a friend. Think about what you like in a friend, and be that kind of person to others. This probably will mean showing interest in other people and being a good listener—all of us want friends who will listen carefully to what we say and take us seriously. To have a friend, be a friend!

KEY VERSE: *Do for others what you would like them to do for you. This is a summary of all that is taught in the law and the prophets. (Matthew 7:12)*

RELATED VERSES: *Romans 12:10; Philippians 2:4*

NOTE TO PARENTS: *If your children ask how to make friends, use this opportunity to teach social skills. Try to find out what's behind the question. Perhaps, as their social circles widen, your children may be worried about losing friends. Or they may be feeling lonely. Start by reassuring them that having trouble making friends is a problem that can be solved. They just need to learn how to do it.*

Q: WHEN YOU'RE MAKING FRIENDS, HOW DO YOU KNOW WHAT TO SAY?

A: The best way to start a conversation with someone is to ask questions about that person. You can look for visible clues on the person to help you know what to ask. For example, if the person is wearing a hat or shirt of a professional sports team, you could ask about the team. If someone is holding a book, you could ask what it's about. It's important to ask people questions about themselves. Talk about them, not just about yourself. Also, look for ways to compliment people. If you hear about a good grade or honor that someone received, you could say, "Good going!" or "Great job!" If someone did well in a concert, you could say something like, "I really enjoyed your solo." Look for ways to give sincere compliments. Try to make others feel good about themselves.

KEY VERSE: *Kind words are like honey—sweet to the soul and healthy for the body. (Proverbs 16:24)*

RELATED VERSES: *Proverbs 22:11; Romans 15:2*

NOTE TO PARENTS: *You can teach your children how to begin conversations by role-playing with them. This will be fun and will give them valuable practice. Also, be sure to model the above advice in your own relationships with your children and with others.*

Q: I WANT TO HAVE NICE FRIENDS, BUT HOW DO I KNOW IF KIDS ARE NICE?

A: You can get an idea of what a person is like by reputation, especially if the reputation is good. For example, if you hear from a lot of people that someone is nice, that's probably a good sign that the person really *is* nice. Sometimes, however, a person's reputation is not always accurate. For example, someone may say that a boy is stuck-up when, instead, he is only shy. Be careful not to judge kids before you know them—give them a chance.

The best way to know if kids are nice is to get to know them yourself. Start talking with them. The Bible teaches that a person's words show what is in that person's heart. If people talk about bad things, swear, or tell dirty jokes, that is a sign of what they are really like. Watch kids in action with others. Pretty soon you will know if they're nice or not.

KEY VERSE: *Many will say they are loyal friends, but who can find one who is really faithful? (Proverbs 20:6)*

RELATED VERSE: *Proverbs 17:17*

NOTE TO PARENTS: *Have fun with this one. Look at magazine pictures and ask your kids what they think the people in the pictures are like. Then you can discuss how looks often deceive and how important it is to get to know a person.*

You may need to help your children identify the types of words and actions that show whether or not someone is nice. Since kids these days are used to hearing bad or unkind words, they may say something like, "Oh, he talks like that, but he's really a nice person." Help your children recognize words as a gauge to a person's heart.

Q: WHERE CAN I FIND SOME FRIENDS?

A: Potential friends are everywhere, usually pretty close by. One of the best places to look for friends is in a group or activity. If you play soccer or sing in choir, for example, you probably will find friends there. Or someone who sits near you in class might turn out to be a good friend. Also consider your church and neighborhood. You might look for someone who needs a friend just as you do. Maybe there's a new family in your neighborhood or church with a child your age. Or maybe you've seen a new student in school. People like that need friends. Perhaps you can be a friend to them.

KEY VERSE: *Anyone who fears you is my friend—anyone who obeys your commandments. (Psalm 119:63)*

RELATED VERSE: *Psalm 55:14*

NOTE TO PARENTS: *Help your children enlarge their friendship circles; plug them in to positive groups. For example, church offers many opportunities for social activities—Bible clubs, choirs, and so on. In addition, you can help by opening your house to other children. Make your home a place where kids want to be.*

Q: WHAT SHOULD I DO IF I'M SCARED TO GO UP TO SOMEONE AND SAY, "HI, DO YOU WANT TO BE MY FRIEND?"

A: You don't have to do that. In fact, that's not a very good way to make friends. That question really puts people on the spot, and they don't know how to answer. It's better to go slower and work at getting to know a person. You can do this by asking them questions about themselves. Let friendship happen; don't force it.

KEY VERSE: *Love each other with genuine affection, and take delight in honoring each other. (Romans 12:10)*

NOTE TO PARENTS: *This is another good place to role-play or practice. You can also tell your children how you make friends.*

Q: WHY CAN'T I HAVE EVERYONE AS A FRIEND?

6

A: There are too many kids and not enough time for you to be a good friend to everyone. Actually, there are many different kinds of friendships. Some friends who are very close will be your very good friends. Some kids, however, you will just know by name; they are called acquaintances. Even if you don't know someone's name, you can be friendly to that person. It's good to like everybody and be friendly, but don't expect everyone to like you the same way and to be a really close friend. Friendship takes time. It takes a lot of talking with someone to know someone well. Be friendly with everyone, but work at having a few very close friends. Keep in mind that even Jesus, who loved everyone, had just three very special friends.

KEY VERSE: *Jesus took Peter, James, and John to the top of a mountain. No one else was there. (Mark 9:2)*

RELATED VERSES: *Matthew 26:37-38*

NOTE TO PARENTS: *Children who ask this question may feel insecure, realizing that not everyone wants to be their friend. Explain the various levels of friendship (acquaintance, friend, close friend, very close friend, etc.), and give examples from your life of friends at each level. Some children will easily develop a few close friendships and tend not to socialize beyond them. Others will easily have many friends, but they may not be close friends. Both casual acquaintances and close friends are helpful and bring happiness to our lives. It's natural to lean one way or the other, but we should help our children develop in both areas.*

Q: WHY DO SOME KIDS NOT WANT TO HAVE FRIENDS?

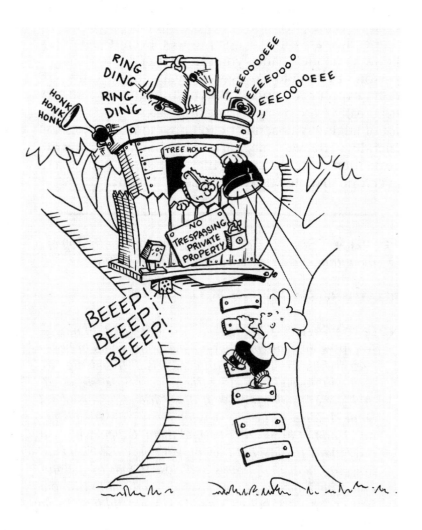

7

A: They may be shy. Or they may be afraid. It can be scary to meet new people if you don't know how. They may be new to the school or neighborhood. And some kids just like to do things by themselves instead of with others. They may have had bad experiences with other kids rejecting them or making fun of them. If this has happened, they may not want to try again. It may seem that some don't want to have friends, but perhaps you just don't know them very well. Maybe you can be a friend to them.

KEY VERSE: *But the time is coming—in fact, it is already here—when you will be scattered, each one going his own way, leaving me alone. Yet I am not alone because the Father is with me. (John 16:32)*

RELATED QUESTIONS: *How does it feel to have no friends? Do loners try to make friends?*

NOTE TO PARENTS: *Maybe your children have been rebuffed in their attempts to befriend other kids. If this is the case, encourage them to continue to be friendly toward those kids but to look for closer friends elsewhere.*

Q: HOW SHOULD I TREAT KIDS WHO ARE DIFFERENT?

8

A: Kids differ in many ways. They may be different races, come from different cultures, or be different sizes. Some children may be mentally or physically challenged. People in a school or neighborhood may even speak different languages. It's never right to make fun of people or ignore them because of those differences. Just because kids are different doesn't mean that they are wrong or to be feared. Think about this: It's God who made the different races and gave people the ability to do things differently. Even if people have different ideas about God, he still wants us to be kind and to respect others. No matter how different kids are, God wants us to treat them in the way we would like to be treated.

KEY VERSE: *The woman was surprised, for Jews refuse to have anything to do with Samaritans. She said to Jesus, "You are a Jew, and I am a Samaritan woman. Why are you asking me for a drink?" (John 4:9)*

RELATED VERSES: *Matthew 25:37-40; Luke 19:1-5*

RELATED QUESTIONS: *Why won't some kids play with kids who are different or who have problems? Why do some kids have to be in wheelchairs?*

NOTE TO PARENTS: *Schools and communities vary. Some are homogenous; others diverse. Every school will have children who are quite different from the others. So be prepared for this question. Also, help your children enjoy and experience the diversity in your community. Take them out for ethnic food. Point out good things in other cultures. Take them to visit special-needs patients in a hospital. The more you help your children experience the differences, the more comfortable they will be with them.*

Q: WHY DO PARENTS NOT LIKE YOUR FRIENDS JUST BECAUSE THEY HAVE GREEN HAIR OR SOMETHING?

9

A: Parents want the best for their children. They know that friends have a big influence. So when they see green hair, they may be surprised or shocked and not know what to think. They know that having green hair may be one way kids express themselves or get attention. But it may also be their way of rebelling against their parents. Your mom and dad probably won't assume that you will want to have green hair too, but they may think that you will pick up your friend's bad attitude. It's not the clothes or hair that your parents don't like; it's what they think the clothes mean to that person. What kind of impression do you give other parents by the way *you* look or act?

KEY VERSE: *Don't copy the behavior and customs of this world, but let God transform you into a new person by changing the way you think. (Romans 12:2)*

RELATED QUESTION: *When kids look tough, why do parents think that they are tough and aren't nice?*

NOTE TO PARENTS: *It's important to get to know your kids' friends. Be careful not to judge them simply by their appearance. Invite the friends to your house. If you notice bad language, bad attitudes, or other negative tendencies, discuss those with your children. Don't make a big issue about appearance unless it becomes evident that it's an outward sign of an inward problem.*

Q: WHY DON'T PARENTS JUST LET YOU PICK YOUR OWN FRIENDS?

10

A: Most parents try to let their children choose their own friends, but some of the choices may not seem very good. Your parents usually know more about your friends' families than you do, and they want you to hang around good and positive moms, dads, brothers, and sisters in other families. Talk this over with your parents. God gave you your parents for a reason. They know you well. Your parents can help you find good friends.

KEY VERSE: *Listen, my child, to what your father teaches you. Don't neglect your mother's teaching. (Proverbs 1:8)*

RELATED VERSES: *Proverbs 13:1; Ephesians 6:1-3*

NOTE TO PARENTS: *Don't be afraid to be involved in helping your children find the right friends. Don't choose for them, but give them guidance. If they really want to befriend someone who is not a good choice for a close friend, that child can still be an acquaintance whom they see from time to time.*

Q:

SOMETIMES WHEN I HANG AROUND WITH MY FRIENDS, THEY DO SOMETHING BAD. WHAT SHOULD I DO?

11

A: If the kids you are with begin to talk about or plan something that is not right, tell them not to do it, firmly but nicely. Don't yell or get angry—just explain that what they are doing is wrong. You can suggest doing something else. If that doesn't work, you should leave. If those kids don't want to be friends anymore or if they continue to do things that are wrong, then they aren't very good friends or the type of friends to have. When something like this happens, be sure to discuss it with your parents.

KEY VERSE: *Whoever walks with the wise will become wise; whoever walks with fools will suffer harm. (Proverbs 13:20)*

RELATED VERSES: *John 17:15; Ephesians 5:11; 3 John 1:11*

RELATED QUESTION: *How do you know if you fit in with all the people in your group?*

NOTE TO PARENTS: *Let your children know that they can talk to you about things like this. Tell them you won't assume that they're bad, too, and you are happy to know that they want to do what's right. When they do come to you, emphasize what they did right more than how bad their friends are. Seeking your advice demonstrates the maturity your children have to make the right friendship decisions on their own, with a little guidance from you.*

Q: WHAT SHOULD I DO WHEN MY OLD FRIENDS DON'T LIKE MY NEW FRIENDS?

12

A: You can't control other people's feelings, so you can't make one person like someone else. Maybe your old friends don't know your new friends—you can help them get acquainted. If one group of friends criticizes the other, you can stick up for those who are being criticized. That's the sign of a real friend. Don't let yourself be drawn into rejecting one group of friends for another—it's all right to have more than one group of friends. You can have friends at church, friends at school, friends who are relatives, and friends in your neighborhood.

KEY VERSES: *But when Peter arrived back in Jerusalem, some of the Jewish believers criticized him. "You entered the home of Gentiles and even ate with them!" they said. (Acts 11:2-3)*

RELATED VERSES: *Proverbs 27:10; Acts 11:1-18; Galatians 2:11-16*

RELATED QUESTION: *How do you know your old friends still like you when you have new friends?*

NOTE TO PARENTS: *Friendships change, and that can be tough for children. It's painful to see relationships fade, whatever the reasons. Changes often occur when new children move into a neighborhood. Even greater changes will take place when your children enter middle school and when they begin high school. Encourage your children to learn now not to give in to pressure to reject new friends. Give them suggestions for ways to be friendly to both old and new friends.*

CLOSER THAN A BROTHER

Being a Good Friend

Q: WHAT'S THE DIFFERENCE BETWEEN BEING BEST FRIENDS AND JUST BEING FRIENDS?

13

A: "Best friends" is a way of saying "very close friends." The difference between "very close friends" and others is that you spend a lot of time with very close friends and you can talk to them about lots of things. Very close friends stick with you when you are having problems or are in a bad mood. You can have a lot of friends, but you'll probably have just a few very close friends. You should be careful about the kinds of kids you choose as your very close friends. They should want to please God and do what is right—like you do. It's hard to be close friends with kids if you and they don't see life the same way.

KEY VERSE: *After David had finished talking with Saul, he met Jonathan, the king's son. There was an immediate bond of love between them, and they became the best of friends. (1 Samuel 18:1)*

RELATED VERSES: *Proverbs 27:6, 17*

NOTE TO PARENTS: *Someone may be one of your children's best friends one week and then somebody else's best friend the next. Be available to give advice and support whenever you discover that your children are negotiating friendships. Encourage them to invite Christian friends over, and try to say yes to activities or outings that involve these children. You can be more sparing with other approvals, but don't always say no. And be sure to always explain your reasoning.*

Q: CAN YOU HAVE MORE THAN ONE BEST FRIEND?

14

A: Of course, if *best* really means "best," then the answer is no. Only one can be the absolute best at anything. But *best* friend usually means *very close* friend. In that case, yes, you can have several very close friends. Try not to single out one person as your one and only *best* friend. Calling a person that may make your other close friends feel bad and think that you don't like them. Just because kids aren't your very closest friends doesn't mean that you can't or shouldn't be friendly to them or spend time with them. Who knows, they might become close friends too.

KEY VERSE: *A friend is always loyal, and a brother is born to help in time of need. (Proverbs 17:17)*

RELATED VERSE: *Galatians 6:10*

NOTE TO PARENTS: *We tend to overuse extremes and superlatives like best. Encourage your children to have more than one close friend instead of narrowing down their friendships to one best friend. Also help your children realize that a circle of close friends shouldn't become an exclusive circle of friends.*

Q: MY FRIEND'S PARENTS ARE GETTING A DIVORCE. WHAT CAN I DO?

15

A: Be a good friend—listen to your friend and give your support. Pray for your friend and his or her parents. Remember, you can't do anything about the parents' relationship with each other. They will have to work that out. You probably don't know much about what has been going on in your friend's family, and that's OK. Being a friend means just being there to talk, listen, and care. Right now your friend really needs you.

KEY VERSE: *I would speak in a way that helps you. I would try to take away your grief. (Job 16:5)*

RELATED VERSES: *Job 2:11; Psalm 35:14; Proverbs 27:9*

NOTE TO PARENTS: *When divorce happens to other families, your children may wonder if it will happen to your family. Assure them of your commitment to Christ and to each other, explaining that you intend to remain married—they don't have to worry.*

Q: WHY DO FRIENDS GET MAD AT YOU WHEN YOU TELL THE TRUTH?

16

A: Truth hurts, especially when someone points out something wrong in our life. Sometimes telling the truth to friends can make them feel very uncomfortable. But just because something is true doesn't mean you have to say it. In fact, sometimes you might think that you're "telling the truth" when you're really just bragging. For example, you may find yourself saying something like, "I'm a better singer than you are." Don't do that—don't compare yourself to others. Instead, look for truthful ways to compliment your friends.

You should be sensitive to others' feelings. There's a right time and a wrong time to speak the truth. If you have an important and possibly painful message, wait to tell your friend in private instead of in front of everyone. Also, the *way* you say something means as much as *what* you say. Always remember to be kind and gentle.

KEY VERSE: *Instead, we will hold to the truth in love, becoming more and more in every way like Christ, who is the head of his body, the church. (Ephesians 4:15)*

RELATED VERSES: *2 Samuel 12:1-12; Proverbs 27:6; Ecclesiastes 3:7*

RELATED QUESTION: *Why can't you lie to your friends?*

NOTE TO PARENTS: *This is a good opportunity to explain tact and the loving use of truth versus the hurtful use of truth. Hurtful truths usually are said during an argument. Help your children understand that it's all right to disagree with someone, but we need to disagree agreeably and lovingly.*

Q:

WHEN YOU ARE TALKING WITH PEOPLE, HOW DO YOU KNOW THAT THEY ARE ACTUALLY LISTENING TO YOU?

17

A: People who listen carefully to you look at you when you are talking—they don't look at the TV or other people. Also, they usually will comment on what you are saying. If you want to make sure that someone is listening, ask a question from time to time about what you have been saying. You could ask, for example, "What do you think?" If someone says, "What?" or "Huh?", you know that the person has not been listening.

Everyone likes to talk to people who know how to listen. Here are three steps to being a good listener: (1) LOOK—stop what you are doing and look at the person who is talking to you. Give that person all of your attention. (2) LISTEN—concentrate on what the person is saying and try to understand. Don't interrupt. (3) RESPOND—say something related to what the person has been talking about. Comment or ask a question; don't just grunt and change the topic.

What kind of listener are you?

KEY VERSES: *My child, listen to me and treasure my instructions. Tune your ears to wisdom, and concentrate on understanding. (Proverbs 2:1-2)*

RELATED VERSES: *Ezekiel 33:30-31; Luke 19:45-48*

NOTE TO PARENTS: *Consider how well you listen to your children. When you talk with them, be sure to look at them and not interrupt. Then comment on what they are saying. Give them your full attention. Be a good example by following the points mentioned above.*

Q: WHY DO FRIENDS TALK BEHIND YOUR BACK?

18

A: Every person is sinful, so everyone does things that are wrong. Sometimes we even harm the people we love. It hurts when friends do that to each other, but it happens.

Most kids who say bad things about others don't realize that it's wrong and hurtful. They have never learned that they are not only hurting others, they are also hurting themselves by pushing friends away. Some kids give in to pressure from others and go along with what has been said, even if it's about a friend. Many times kids will repeat things they've heard about someone without talking to the person to see if those things are true. This is known as gossiping. Spreading rumors can really hurt people. The Bible says gossiping is wrong—it hurts people and breaks up friendships.

KEY VERSE: *For I am afraid that when I come to visit you I won't like what I find, and then you won't like my response. I am afraid that I will find quarreling, jealousy, outbursts of anger, selfishness, backstabbing, gossip, conceit, and disorderly behavior. (2 Corinthians 12:20)*

RELATED VERSES: *Psalm 41:7; Proverbs 16:28; 18:24; Romans 1:29-30*

RELATED QUESTIONS: *Why do friends tell mean secrets about you? Why can't my friends just tell me everything they know?*

NOTE TO PARENTS: *What kind of example do you set? Be careful not to gossip. A good time to teach your children the difference between gossiping and reporting facts is when they tell you about some trouble between them and another child. Teach your children how to report facts without making judgments.*

Q: WHY WON'T MY FRIEND LET ME PLAY WITH HIS STUFF?

19

A: Your friend may be afraid that his stuff will be broken or misused. Maybe someone recently played with one of his toys and broke it. Remember, the stuff belongs to your friend, so respect his wishes. If you want to play with your friend's things, ask him and promise to take good care of it. If he lets you, show him how careful you can be. If he says no, don't keep asking. Let it go.

KEY VERSE: *Show respect for everyone. Love your Christian brothers and sisters. Fear God. (1 Peter 2:17)*

NOTE TO PARENTS: *Explain to your children that although people are more important than possessions, misusing someone's property can destroy a relationship. The key is to respect the friend. Showing respect to a friend involves respecting that person's property. On the other hand, encourage your children to be willing to share their things. "I'm afraid they might break it" can be an excuse for selfishness.*

Q: WHY CAN'T I GO OVER TO MY BEST FRIEND'S HOUSE VERY OFTEN?

I HAVE SWIMMING LESSONS ON MONDAYS, VIOLIN LESSONS TUESDAYS, GYMNASTICS ON WEDNESDAYS, CUBS ON THURSDAYS, AND FRIDAY IS MY INTERNET NIGHT. BUT I CAN FIT YOU IN BETWEEN A DENTIST APPOINTMENT AND MY PAPER ROUTE SATURDAY MORNING... I ALWAYS MAKE TIME FOR MY BEST FRIEND!

20

A: If your parents are saying that you can't go over to your friend's house very often, ask them why. Maybe they don't know your friend very well. You can fix that by having your friend come to your house. If your friend doesn't invite you very often, maybe it's because the parents won't allow it. They may have several reasons, so don't blame your friend. Perhaps your friend is busy with other activities and doesn't have much free time.

Of course, it may be that you want to go over to your friend's house every day. If that's the case, your parents probably don't want you to "wear out your welcome."

KEY VERSE: *Don't visit your neighbors too often, or you will wear out your welcome. (Proverbs 25:17)*

RELATED QUESTION: *Why are sleep-overs better than just sleeping by yourself?*

NOTE TO PARENTS: *Teach your children some of the guidelines for moderate and mutually fair hospitality. Double-check your children's knowledge and performance of good manners. Remind them that polite, courteous, and helpful people are pleasant to be around and usually get invited back.*

Q: WHY DON'T MY PARENTS LET ME GO TO SPECIAL PLACES WITH MY FRIENDS?

21

A: What are some places that are special to you? The movie theater? The mall? An arcade? An ice-cream shop? Sometimes a certain place may seem special, but your parents know that bad things can happen there. They will want to know if any adults will be present if you go there, because even a safe place can become dangerous quickly. Because your parents love you, they want to protect you so you won't get hurt or get into trouble. This means they probably won't let you go to many places by yourself or just with your friends. When your parents do let you go to special places, be extra careful to be responsible and obedient. Your parents will probably allow you to do more as they see you becoming more responsible.

KEY VERSE: *Obey your spiritual leaders and do what they say. Their work is to watch over your souls, and they know they are accountable to God. Give them reason to do this joyfully and not with sorrow. That would certainly not be for your benefit. (Hebrews 13:17)*

RELATED VERSE: *Proverbs 22:3*

RELATED QUESTIONS: *Why do other people get special privileges and I don't? Why do friends go to more special places than our family does?*

NOTE TO PARENTS: *As spiritual leaders for our children, sometimes we can be overprotective. Eventually, however, we have to let them go. This process begins when children are young. Show them that you love and trust them by allowing them to venture out to select places with their friends. But make sure that these places are safe and supervised or chaperoned by responsible adults.*

Q: WHY SHOULD WE ALWAYS HAVE TO RESCUE OUR FRIENDS WHEN THEY GET IN TROUBLE?

22

A:

God says that we should help those who are in trouble, even our *enemies*. That's what it means to love, and it's how we can show others God's love. You can help your friends when they are in trouble. That's being a very good friend to them. However, there's a limit to what you can do—parents and other adults may need to help. You shouldn't lie for friends or make excuses for them. Sometimes letting friends learn to solve their own problems is the best thing to do.

KEY VERSE: *The greatest love is shown when people lay down their lives for their friends. (John 15:13)*

RELATED VERSES: *Psalm 107:6; Proverbs 19:19*

RELATED QUESTION: *How can I help when my friend is grounded at home?*

NOTE TO PARENTS: *It's good for your children to learn how to help others, but don't be afraid to step in when friends seem to be taking advantage of your children's goodwill. Kids want to help their friends and will automatically try to defend and protect a child who is in trouble for doing something wrong. Help your children understand that at times they need to rescue their friends, but at other times it is better to let those kids experience the consequences of their actions.*

Q: WHAT SHOULD I DO IF MY FRIEND TURNS ON A SHOW THAT I'M NOT ALLOWED TO WATCH?

23

A:

You can explain that you're not allowed to watch that show and ask your friend to change the channel. If that doesn't work, you can excuse yourself and go to another room or even go home, telling your friend in a nice way how you feel. You can explain why your parents don't want you to watch that show. This may help your friend make wiser choices when it comes to watching television. You may also want to explain that your parents will get very upset if they find out—it's just not worth the risk. Then you can suggest something else to do.

KEY VERSES: *I will refuse to look at anything vile and vulgar. I hate all crooked dealings; I will have nothing to do with them. I will reject perverse ideas and stay away from every evil. (Psalm 101:3-4)*

RELATED VERSES: *Proverbs 1:10; 1 Corinthians 10:13; 2 Timothy 2:22*

RELATED QUESTION: *Why do kids sometimes get nightmares from the movies they watch?*

NOTE TO PARENTS: *Regulating your children's TV watching is easier said than done. Talk about specific TV shows and videos with your children. Let them know your expectations and reasons. Also assure them that at any age and at any time they can call you if a situation gets out of hand, and you will come pick them up.*

UPS
AND
DOWNS

Handling Friendship
Difficulties

Q: WHY DO FRIENDS LET EACH OTHER DOWN?

24

A: Sometimes we expect too much from our friends; then we feel let down when they don't come through for us. Some of our friends may be having a bad day and are working on their own problems. At those times your friends will find it difficult to help you. At other times your friends may not even be aware of your problems. They may not know that they have let you down. It's all right to express your disappointment and explain to them how you feel. When you talk to your friends in a nice way about how you feel, it will help you and them learn how to be better friends.

KEY VERSE: *The godly give good advice to their friends; the wicked lead them astray. (Proverbs 12:26)*

RELATED VERSES: *Proverbs 20:6; Mark 14:44-50; 2 Timothy 4:16*

RELATED QUESTION: *Why do my friends let me down when I'm honest with them?*

NOTE TO PARENTS: *This provides a good opportunity to explain that friendships have ups and downs. That's normal. It's also a good time to encourage your children to have several good friends and not just one best friend.*

Q: IF A FRIEND ASKS ME TO KEEP A PROMISE AND IT'S SOMETHING WRONG, SHOULD I DO IT?

25

A: You don't have to keep a promise if someone will be hurt by it. If your friend says something like, "I'm going to tell you something, but you have to promise not to tell anyone else," you can say, "I can't promise to do that if what you are going to tell me is wrong." Let your friend know that you can't make any promise that goes against your promise to God to obey him. It's better to let your friend know up front what promises you will keep. Then, when you do promise something, be sure to keep your promise.

KEY VERSE: *Take no part in the worthless deeds of evil and darkness; instead, rebuke and expose them. (Ephesians 5:11)*

RELATED QUESTION: *When friends break promises, don't they want to do what they said? or do they sometimes forget?*

NOTE TO PARENTS: *You can model appropriate keeping of promises with your children. Be sure to keep the secrets they share whenever you can. Let your children know, however, that if someone will be hurt, you won't keep quiet.*

Q: WHY CAN'T MY BEST FRIEND STAY HERE WITH ME AND NOT MOVE AWAY?

26

A:

It hurts when friends leave. It hurts your friend even more because, although you are losing one person, your friend is leaving almost everyone familiar. Your friend's family probably had a good reason for moving; for example, a parent may have received a promotion or a new job. Perhaps you can get your friend's new address and continue your friendship as pen pals or E-mail pals. Many families who move away from a city come back to visit. If you stay in touch, you will know when your friend is coming and possibly be able to get together.

Someday *you* might have to move. One of the facts of life is that situations don't stay the same, so it's important to learn how to deal with change.

KEY VERSES: *When he had finished speaking, he knelt and prayed with them. They wept aloud as they embraced him in farewell, sad most of all because he had said that they would never see him again. Then they accompanied him down to the ship. (Acts 20:36-38)*

RELATED VERSE: *2 Timothy 1:4*

RELATED QUESTION: *Is it OK to feel sad when friends leave?*

NOTE TO PARENTS: *Because society has become very mobile, some of your children's friends will probably move away. Instead of focusing on the losses, help your children learn to value the friendships they have. Encourage your children to keep in touch with their long-distance friends through E-mail, phone calls, and letters. If your family will be moving, pray together about the new friendships that will be formed in your new neighborhood, church, and school.*

Q: WHY WOULD YOUR FRIENDS EXPECT YOU TO LIE FOR THEM?

27

A: Some people think that friends should do anything for them—even lie. But that's not part of friendship. More important than doing what your friends want or expect is doing what God wants. That's what you should consider first. Your relationship with God should be your most important friendship, and God says that lying is wrong.

KEY VERSE: *Do not steal. Do not cheat one another. Do not lie. (Leviticus 19:11)*

RELATED VERSE: *Ephesians 4:25*

RELATED QUESTIONS: *Why do we lie to keep friends out of trouble? Why can't my friend just not do anything wrong so I don't have to lie for her?*

NOTE TO PARENTS: *Help your children know that a lie is the "intent to deceive." It's intentionally keeping quiet about the truth. In other words, a lie is not limited to saying words that are untrue. Saying nothing or saying the right words in the wrong way can also be lying.*

Q: WHY DON'T YOUR FRIENDS LIKE YOU JUST FOR WHO YOU ARE?

28

A: Usually they do. That's probably what caused you to become friends in the first place—they like who you are. At times, however, friends may want to change something about who you are that's different from who *they* are. They may want you to stop doing things that are different from what *they* do. One of the great parts of friendship is getting to know someone who is completely different from you. God didn't make any two people alike, so learn to appreciate how your friends are different.

KEY VERSES: *Just as our bodies have many parts and each part has a special function, so it is with Christ's body. We are all parts of his one body, and each of us has different work to do. And since we are all one body in Christ, we belong to each other, and each of us needs all the others. (Romans 12:4-5)*

RELATED VERSE: *Romans 12:2*

RELATED QUESTION: *Why do friends expect you to do things just the way they do?*

NOTE TO PARENTS: *Kids face pressure to conform. Help them be true to themselves without being weird. Encourage your children to accept constructive criticism and to change when their friends bring up something that they perhaps should change.*

Q: WHY DO YOU HAVE TO DO WHATEVER YOUR FRIENDS WANT, OR THEY GET MAD?

29

A: It's natural to want to have our own way, so your friends may get mad at you when you don't do something they want you to do. That's not the way friendship should work, however. Sometimes a compromise is the way for everyone to be happy. Other times it means taking turns doing what each friend wants. If friends always want things their way or if they get angry with you when you don't conform, talk with them about it. If your friends are pressuring you to do something that you aren't comfortable with or that is dangerous or wrong, then you probably should find a new set of friends.

KEY VERSES: *Keep away from angry, short-tempered people, or you will learn to be like them and endanger your soul. (Proverbs 22:24-25)*

RELATED VERSES: *Ecclesiastes 7:9; 1 Corinthians 13:4-5*

NOTE TO PARENTS: *Help your children think about times when it's appropriate to give in to others and times when it's important not to give in to them, even if they get angry.*

Q: WHY CAN'T FRIENDS JUST GET ALONG INSTEAD OF FIGHTING AND ARGUING WITH EACH OTHER?

30

A: You'd think that friends would get along great *all the time*. But conflicts happen because everyone has ups and downs; sometimes a person is just in a bad mood. No two people agree on everything all the time. In any disagreement, however, instead of fighting and arguing, the people should talk it through and work together to solve the problem. If your friends are always fighting and arguing, you can be a good example yourself and help them resolve the issue. And you can keep from following the bad example of your friends by spending more time with kids who are learning to get along with each other.

KEY VERSE: *Beginning a quarrel is like opening a floodgate, so drop the matter before a dispute breaks out. (Proverbs 17:14)*

RELATED VERSE: *Proverbs 20:3*

RELATED QUESTIONS: *Why can't you tell on a friend without your friendship breaking up? What do you do if friends fight and argue with each other? Should you leave if your friends are in a fight?*

NOTE TO PARENTS: *A good place to teach children how to get along with others is at home as they deal with their brothers and sisters. Enabling your children to work out sibling conflicts takes time. But it's an important way for them to develop the skills they need to get along with each other and with their friends. When arguments occur, teach your children how to "fight fair." Let them know it is possible to disagree with someone without screaming, yelling, and calling them names.*

Q: WHY DO MY FRIENDS BREAK THEIR PROMISES TO ME?

31

A: Only God is perfect and will never break his promises. Most people who make promises intend to keep them, but they may forget. Or circumstances may change. For example, a friend may say that you can visit her anytime, but a baby brother arrives and the family limits the number of visitors for a while. Sometimes people make promises that are almost impossible to keep—like saying, "I will never get angry with you." If a friend breaks a promise to you, let that person know how you feel, but try to be forgiving and understanding. Ask God to help you make only promises that you can keep. Then do your best to keep those promises.

KEY VERSE: *It is better to say nothing than to promise something that you don't follow through on. (Ecclesiastes 5:5)*

RELATED VERSES: *1 Kings 8:23; Proverbs 17:17*

RELATED QUESTION: *Instead of making promises they'll break, why won't friends just be quiet?*

NOTE TO PARENTS: *When children discover the promise concept, they can overuse it to make pacts with their friends. Help your children understand that promises are important and that we should say what we mean and do what we say.*

32

A: Don't join in. Maybe you could change the subject or get your friend to do something else instead. If things get bad, remember that no one has the right to touch or hit another person if that person doesn't want them to. Adults who hit people can go to jail for their actions. It's against the law, and it's not the way God wants us to treat others. If your friend's actions involve pushing or hitting of any kind, tell him to stop. Then go tell an adult immediately.

KEY VERSE: *Dear friend, don't let this bad example influence you. Follow only what is good. (3 John 1:11)*

RELATED VERSES: *Luke 6:37; 1 Corinthians 13:4-5*

RELATED QUESTIONS: *Why do people have to tease and not be friends? If a friend is mean to other people, should I be his or her best friend?*

NOTE TO PARENTS: *This is an answer that's easy to say, but hard to do. Your child may need backup from you. With all the violence that children see on television and in movies, they may think that mild physical abuse is part of life. Respect for others begins at home. Teach your children to respect others' rights for safety. Never allow any touching with the intent to harm.*

Q: IF MY FRIENDS IGNORE ME, SHOULD I IGNORE THEM?

33

A: No—we should do what is right toward others even if they do wrong to us. This is difficult, but God expects us to do what is right regardless of what others do. Over time, our friendliness may win the other kids over. Sometimes we should just overlook what people do to us, but we should not ignore them as people. Probably the best way to act toward someone who is ignoring you is the exact opposite. You can go right up to the person and say something like this: "I'm sorry if I have upset you. Can we talk about it?"

KEY VERSE: *Never pay back evil for evil to anyone. Do things in such a way that everyone can see you are honorable. (Romans 12:17)*

RELATED VERSE: *Psalm 66:20*

RELATED QUESTIONS: *Sometimes people I talk to listen for a second, then the next minute they're ignoring me. Why do people do this? When friends aren't friendly anymore, should I ask them, "Why are you ignoring me?"*

NOTE TO PARENTS: *This issue can be a crisis for children. You may say, "Just ignore anyone who ignores you." But the hurt will still be there. Friendships change over time, and even the strongest ones experience stress. Talking with someone who doesn't want to talk is not a natural thing to do. However, if you can help your children through it a couple of times until they see positive results, they will develop it as a life habit.*

Q: WHY DO SOME PEOPLE WANT TO BE FRIENDS ONE DAY AND NOT THE NEXT?

34

A: Learning how to be a good friend takes time and effort. Your friends may not realize that the way they are behaving is wrong. Nicely talk with them about it and how it makes you feel. Explain that you would like to know you can count on your friends every day.

It is possible that some kids may *seem* like they're changing their mind about being friends, but they may just be having a bad day. Or they may be spending time that day with another friend. If that's the case, don't worry; they are still your friends.

KEY VERSE: *Never abandon a friend. (Proverbs 27:10)*

NOTE TO PARENTS: *Sometimes children can be possessive about friendships and want to monopolize a person's time and attention. But that will suffocate any friendship. If you think that's happening, help your child understand the importance of developing other friendships as well.*

Q:
WHAT CAN I DO WHEN ONE OF MY BEST FRIENDS USED TO LIKE ME, BUT NOW HE HATES ME?

35

A: First, try to find out what happened. Did you do something to hurt your friend's feelings? If you find out that you did, say that you're sorry. Pray about the situation and ask God for wisdom. Remember, however, that there just may not be a good reason— people change, and you may have lost a friend. Don't try to get even and don't decide to dislike the person back. You can still be nice and pray for your old friend, but be sure to find other friends.

KEY VERSE: *My friends scorn me, but I pour out my tears to God. (Job 16:20)*

RELATED VERSE: *Proverbs 18:19*

RELATED QUESTION: *If kids don't want to be friends anymore, is it OK to just forget about them?*

NOTE TO PARENTS: *Children will often use the word hate when referring to a former friend. What they usually mean is that they are upset with the person. A number of things can spoil a friendship. When relationships sour, there's a tendency to try to "get even." Instead, encourage your children to see this as a good opportunity to become more like Jesus, showing kindness even when it's not returned.*

ROCKY ROAD

Learning to Get Along with Others

Q: WHY ARE SOME KIDS SO MESSY?

36

A:

Kids are different. Some are neat, some are messy, and some are in between. Also, every family is different; some keep their homes much neater than others. So a person who grows up in a messy home may tend to be messy. It's good to be tidy and organized, and hopefully your messy friends will learn this as they grow up. But we shouldn't expect everyone to have everything perfectly in order all the time. While a messy person can be frustrating for someone who is neat, we should remember that being neat is not the most important thing in life. If some people aren't as neat as we are, that doesn't mean that they're bad—just different.

KEY VERSE: *Are we not all children of the same Father? Are we not all created by the same God? (Malachi 2:10)*

RELATED QUESTIONS: *Why do kids lose so many things? If my friends are messy, should I try to help them out or remind them to pick up after themselves?*

NOTE TO PARENTS: *It's easy to get into the habit of seeing others' weaknesses. This habit will frustrate us and divide friends. Help your children work on their own weaknesses and focus on others' strengths. This habit will mature them and strengthen their friendships.*

Q: WHY DO SOME KIDS GET THEIR OWN WAY WHEN THEY CRY AND GET ANGRY?

37

A: Some adults give in when children cry, pout, whine, or throw tantrums. The adults let those children get what they want. Kids who have been treated that way think they can always get what they want by acting like that. But someday those actions won't work. Can you imagine adults falling to the floor in a store, crying loudly, and beating the floor just because the store didn't have what they wanted? It's much better to learn as children to talk things through, be cooperative, and not try to get our way all the time.

KEY VERSES: *So Samson's wife came to him in tears and said, "You don't love me; you hate me! You have given my people a riddle, but you haven't told me the answer." "I haven't even given the answer to my father or mother," he replied. "Why should I tell you?" So she cried whenever she was with him and kept it up for the rest of the celebration. At last, on the seventh day, he told her the answer because of her persistent nagging. Then she gave the answer to the young men. (Judges 14:16-17)*

RELATED QUESTION: *Why do some kids always want their own way?*

NOTE TO PARENTS: *If your children point out that some friends get their way by throwing tantrums, help your kids understand that every home is unique. You are doing your best before God to be a good parent to your family in your home. No one should worry about whether or not other families are different or better. Talk about the fact that when someone in your family is disappointed over something, everyone can get together to work out a happy alternative.*

Q: WHY DO SOME KIDS ALWAYS TRY TO BE FIRST?

ICE CREAM

38

A: They're selfish. And, by the way, that's part of the sinful, human nature. *All* people tend to be selfish. Only God can help us be unselfish and think of others—we have to depend on him. Kids who always try to be first may be trying to feel better about themselves. They may feel that they are important and valuable because they won a game or got to be first in line. But God says that each person is valuable and important to him, even those who come in last. When we know how much God loves and cares for us, we can let others go first.

KEY VERSE: *And so it is, that many who are first now will be last then; and those who are last now will be first then. (Matthew 20:16)*

RELATED VERSES: *Philippians 2:3-4; James 3:16*

NOTE TO PARENTS: *We should encourage our children to do their best, and it's certainly not wrong to win a game or contest. The problem comes when winning becomes everything. In small matters, like lining up for the drinking fountain, help your children learn that God is happier when we don't try to be first all the time.*

Q: SHOULD I STAND UP FOR MYSELF AROUND PUSHY KIDS?

39

A: Yes, tell them how you feel. Be firm, but don't yell and lose your cool. The Bible says that a gentle answer will help calm a situation. Staying cool and being as nice as you can is your best chance for a good outcome. Sometimes this won't work, and you'll be tempted to fight. But don't do it—walk away instead. If kids get pushy, tell an adult.

***

KEY VERSE: *A gentle answer turns away wrath, but harsh words stir up anger. (Proverbs 15:1)*

RELATED VERSES: *Nehemiah 6:8-9; Matthew 5:39*

RELATED QUESTIONS: *Why do I get upset around friends who are pushy? Should I tell pushy kids not to be pushy because no one likes it?*

NOTE TO PARENTS: *Many parents tell their children to stand up for themselves and push back. But the Bible says to honor others and to turn the other cheek. This doesn't mean that children should become doormats. They should stand up for their rights but do it respectfully. They shouldn't fight.*

Q:

WHY DO SOME KIDS JUST HAVE TO TALK IN CLASS? WHY CAN'T THEY WAIT UNTIL RECESS?

40

A: Some are not mature enough to wait. Babies can't wait for anything. They want to be changed or fed or moved *now!* As children get older, however, they learn to have patience and do things at the right time, not whenever they feel like it. They also learn that the whole world doesn't revolve around them and that other people have needs too. Some kids, however, take a little longer than they should to learn these lessons.

Some kids might talk in class because they're afraid they will forget what they have to say. You could suggest that they write a reminder note to themselves to talk about it at recess or between classes.

KEY VERSE: *Don't talk too much, for it fosters sin. Be sensible and turn off the flow! (Proverbs 10:19)*

RELATED VERSES: *Proverbs 20:19; Ecclesiastes 3:1, 7; James 3:2*

RELATED QUESTIONS: *If kids talk during class, should I tell them it's not polite? When the teacher asks a student a question, why do some other kids always call out the answer?*

NOTE TO PARENTS: *If your children talk too much, encourage them to work on this. Discuss possible solutions with their teachers.*

Q: WHY DO KIDS WRECK MY THINGS FOR NO REASON?

41

A: Some kids are careless, and they break things by accident. Some are stronger than they realize and may not know what they are doing. Of course, some may be mean and break your things to hurt you. Some have never learned to take care of other people's property. Let your friends know that you expect them to be careful with your things. You don't have to let kids play with your toys if you know those kids don't care how they handle your things. You don't have to let people into your room if you know they don't care if they mess it up. Be careful, however, not to overreact to a small incident or an accident. Sharing is an important part of friendship.

KEY VERSE: *Let everyone see that you are considerate in all you do. (Philippians 4:5)*

RELATED VERSE: *Ephesians 4:2*

RELATED QUESTIONS: *Do some kids wreck things because they think they're not going to get caught? If friends lose or break my things, why can't I just make them replace those things?*

NOTE TO PARENTS: *Some kids may be mean and cruel. You have to help your children draw the line between sharing and protecting their stuff from careless kids. Be careful what you teach about ownership. Teach your children to respect others' ownership but also to be willing to share what they own.*

Q: WHY DO SOME KIDS ACT TOUGH?

42

A: Usually kids who act tough are trying hard to feel good about themselves. They want everyone to look up to them the way people look up to entertainment or sports celebrities. Tough kids might be nice if they would just start being themselves. And kids who act important would have a lot more friends if they didn't pretend to be better than everyone else. The best person to be is yourself. Then when people like you, you will know that they like you for who you are and not for a pretend image that you are trying to have.

KEY VERSE: *Live in harmony with each other. Don't try to act important, but enjoy the company of ordinary people. And don't think you know it all! (Romans 12:16)*

RELATED VERSES: *Luke 18:9-14; Romans 12:3; 1 Corinthians 4:7; Galatians 2:6*

RELATED QUESTION: *Do kids try to act tough just to attract attention?*

NOTE TO PARENTS: *All kids need attention, and they need to feel good about themselves. We should look for ways to affirm our children, always being ready to give them positive feedback. Don't be afraid that this will make them act important. Instead, children who are confident that they are loved, accepted, and special to their families as well as to God find it much easier to act natural. They know it's OK to be themselves.*

Q: WHY DO SOME KIDS SAY BAD THINGS ABOUT OTHERS?

43

A: They think it's fun. They might be jealous of other kids or angry with them. They might be in competition with them. Or they may not have learned yet that it's unkind. Whatever the reason, it's not right to say bad things about people, to call them names, to spread rumors, or to make fun of others. Unfortunately a lot of humor these days is based on making fun of someone. But laughing at someone is a cruel way to joke around. Don't do it. A good rule to follow is to make sure that everything you say about people will make them feel good. Pretend that they are present to hear what you're saying about them, even if they're not.

KEY VERSE: *They must not speak evil of anyone, and they must avoid quarreling. Instead, they should be gentle and show true humility to everyone. (Titus 3:2)*

RELATED VERSES: *Matthew 12:36; 1 Peter 4:4*

RELATED QUESTIONS: *What should I do if someone says bad things about my friend? When kids talk bad about others, does it always mean they don't like those people?*

NOTE TO PARENTS: *Kids can be cruel to each other. Their cutting remarks often relate to a physical characteristic or other superficial attribute, such as clothing. In addition to helping your children see how unkind it is to put others down, encourage them to look beyond the superficial to the real person. Remember that your children are listening when you talk about others. Making cutting remarks and put-down jokes is a bad habit, and using sarcasm is a destructive disciplinary tool. Make your home a safe place where your children and their friends feel welcomed and affirmed. You may want to add "saying only kind things about people" to your list of family rules.*

Q: WHY ARE SOME KIDS BULLIES?

A: They are very selfish and care more about themselves than others. Usually bullies are bigger and stronger than other kids and can take advantage of them. They have learned to get what they want by force. Bullies come in all ages. You can find them in many places in the grown-up world as well as on the playground. No one should get away with bullying others. If you see it or get bullied yourself, tell a teacher, the principal, or your parents right away.

KEY VERSES: *Goliath walked out toward David with his shield bearer ahead of him, sneering in contempt at this ruddy-faced boy. (1 Samuel 17:41-42)*

RELATED VERSE: *Ecclesiastes 4:1*

RELATED QUESTIONS: *What should I do if a bully pushes me around all the time? When someone is being a bully, should I complain to a teacher or adult?*

NOTE TO PARENTS: *If your child is being bullied by someone at school, talk to the teacher. If it's someone in the neighborhood, talk to the parent. Your child does not have to endure cruelty from a bully.*

Q: SHOULD I STICK UP FOR SOMEONE WHO'S BEING BULLIED?

45

A: Yes, always stick up for the person who is being hurt, not the one doing the hurting. If there is a big, strong bully at your school or in your neighborhood, you may want to encourage your friends to stay together in a group to be safer. Be sure to tell an adult about the situation too. Let this person know if extra adult supervision is needed on your school playground. If kids don't feel safe walking home from school, parents may be able to take turns giving rides.

KEY VERSE: *I say to the rest of you, dear brothers and sisters, never get tired of doing good. (2 Thessalonians 3:13)*

RELATED VERSES: *Proverbs 21:3; 2 Corinthians 8:21*

RELATED QUESTION: *Should I tell the bully's parents what he's doing?*

NOTE TO PARENTS: *Encourage your child to inform a caring adult about bully action. This could be a coach, a teacher, a parent, a principal, or another caring adult.*

Q:

IF YOU KNOW A FRIEND IS GOING TO DO SOMETHING WRONG, SHOULD YOU TRY TO STOP THE PERSON?

46

A: Yes, definitely. First, try to talk your friend out of doing what is wrong. Explain that you care about him or her and that's why you want to help. Use your friendship to encourage this friend into doing what is right instead of wrong. If he or she won't listen, tell your parents. If you are present when your friend starts to do what is wrong, leave immediately.

KEY VERSE: *Don't think only about your own affairs, but be interested in others, too, and what they are doing. (Philippians 2:4)*

RELATED VERSE: *2 Timothy 4:2*

RELATED QUESTIONS: *What should I do if I have a friend who does wrong things all the time? If my friends do wrong things, should I tell an adult even if I lose those friends?*

NOTE TO PARENTS: *Two kids can handle many issues without outside help. On the other hand, a "wrong" may be destructive and involve dangerous actions such as drinking, experimenting with drugs, vandalism, or shoplifting. In those situations, adults should be involved as soon as possible. Help your children understand the difference.*

Q: WHAT SHOULD I DO WHEN KIDS ARE MEAN TO ME?

47

A: This will be difficult, but you should be kind to them no matter how mean they are to you. Also, you should pray for them. That's what God expects his people to do. God's way always works out best. You may think that you'll feel better by getting even, but you won't. If you respond God's way, you'll feel better about yourself, and you may even help those kids change when they see your good example. If you have to, avoid them. Don't let their meanness get to you. If they threaten to hurt you physically, you should tell an adult right away.

KEY VERSES: *If your enemies are hungry, feed them. If they are thirsty, give them something to drink, and they will be ashamed of what they have done to you. Don't let evil get the best of you, but conquer evil by doing good. (Romans 12:20-21)*

RELATED VERSES: *1 Peter 2:21-23*

RELATED QUESTIONS: *Do you have to walk away to avoid fights? If someone punches me, what should I do?*

NOTE TO PARENTS: *Every child experiences unkind behavior. "Being mean" can involve anything from name-calling and taunting to hurting someone physically. Sometimes kids feel sad or even guilty about being mistreated and, therefore, won't mention it. So it's important that from time to time you ask your children how people are treating them at school and in the neighborhood.*

48

A:

It is very difficult to love enemies because it's not natural. It's the opposite of how everyone around us seems to be behaving. When people hurt us, we want to get back at them because we are human. When people don't like us or act mean toward us, it's natural not to like them. But Jesus tells us to love our enemies, and he promises to give us the strength to do it. "Loving" enemies doesn't necessarily mean having warm feelings about them. It means acting in a loving way toward them, treating them the way Jesus would—praying for them, being kind to them, and so on.

KEY VERSE: *But I say, love your enemies! Pray for those who persecute you! (Matthew 5:44)*

RELATED VERSES: *Luke 6:35-37; Romans 12:17-21*

RELATED QUESTION: *How do you love someone who hates you?*

NOTE TO PARENTS: *Here's another place where you can be a positive example for your children. They are watching you. How do you react when people cut you off in traffic, yell at you, or accuse you falsely? Pray for God's help to respond in love.*

Q: WHEN KIDS TEASE ME, IS IT OK TO TEASE THEM BACK?

49

A: There's a difference between fun teasing and mean teasing. Sometimes kids say nonsense things about each other, not meaning to hurt anyone's feelings. That's OK. When kids tease you in a mean way, however, don't tease them back. Try to ignore them if possible. Just stay quiet. This won't be easy because it's natural to want to say something back to hurt them. If you can, be kind to them. Jesus calls this "turning the other cheek." If a certain group of kids seems to tease you all the time, don't go near those kids. If they call you names, remind yourself that the names do not describe the real you. God knows you, and he says you're special.

KEY VERSE: *Don't repay evil for evil. Don't retaliate when people say unkind things about you. Instead, pay them back with a blessing. That is what God wants you to do, and he will bless you for it. (1 Peter 3:9)*

RELATED VERSES: *Matthew 5:39; 1 Peter 2:21-23*

RELATED QUESTION: *Why do some kids like to tease others?*

NOTE TO PARENTS: *Words can hurt, can't they? They can hurt you, and they can hurt your children. Words can cut and wound deeper than "sticks and stones." Be prepared to heal some word wounds.*

Q: WHY DON'T OTHER KIDS EVER DO WHAT I SAY?

50

A: Do you like to tell others what to do? Do you always want things your way? If that's the case, kids may start ignoring you. Or perhaps some kids don't know you well enough to listen to your suggestions. Your good friends who know you and like you will probably take your ideas and suggestions seriously if you're not too bossy.

Remember, though, no one *has* to do what you say or suggest. You need to learn how to present your ideas in a way that others will want to go along with you. If you support your friends when they have good suggestions, those kids will be a lot easier to convince when you have a good idea.

KEY VERSES: *The next day, as Moses was out visiting his people again, he saw two Hebrew men fighting. "What are you doing, hitting your neighbor like that?" Moses said to the one in the wrong. "Who do you think you are?" the man replied. "Who appointed you to be our prince and judge?" (Exodus 2:13-14)*

RELATED VERSES: *2 Corinthians 1:24; 1 Peter 5:3*

NOTE TO PARENTS: *Children don't develop great social and communication skills automatically. They do, however, often act like their parents. Therefore, if your children talk too much or boss others around, they may have learned that at home. Model and teach good listening skills, and help your children learn how to explain their ideas and suggestions clearly.*

THE "IN" CROWD

Fitting In at School

Q: WHY DO SOME KIDS DRESS SO WEIRD?

51

A: They may like to do it. Actually, their clothes may seem weird to you but not to them. Of course, some kids wear loud and different clothes to be noticed. They want to get a reaction, to get attention. Some kids whose clothes seem weird may be copying musicians or other celebrities who they think are cool. Others may look different just because they don't have enough money to dress in style. Remember not to judge people by the way they dress.

KEY VERSES: *Everything [the Pharisees] do is for show. On their arms they wear extra wide prayer boxes with Scripture verses inside, and they wear extra long tassels on their robes. They enjoy the attention they get on the streets. (Matthew 23:5, 7)*

RELATED VERSE: *1 Samuel 16:7; Matthew 3:4*

RELATED QUESTION: *What should I wear at school?*

NOTE TO PARENTS: *Remember, clothes don't make the person. This cuts both ways. A wonderful person may be dressed in weird clothes. Conversely, a rotten person can hide in the latest styles. It's easy to judge people by their appearance. Be careful to set a good example in this area.*

Q: SOMETIMES I'M AFRAID TO GO TO SCHOOL. WHAT SHOULD I DO?

52

A: Talk to your parents about your fears. They will help. If there's a specific reason why you are afraid, tell them about it. Teachers and school counselors can also help. You may want to go to school with a friend. This friend can encourage you, pray for you, and give you moral support. Also, you can ask Christian friends, such as your Sunday school teacher and pastor, to pray for you. They can pray also that God will take care of the situation that is causing you to be afraid.

KEY VERSE: *I am holding you by your right hand—I, the Lord your God. And I say to you, "Do not be afraid. I am here to help you." (Isaiah 41:13)*

RELATED VERSES: *Psalm 56:3; Isaiah 26:3; 41:10; Philippians 4:6-7*

NOTE TO PARENTS: *Find out why your child is afraid. The first answer may not be the real reason. Instead of telling your son or daughter to be tough, take time to talk it through and find out what's really happening. A bully may be lurking. Kids may be making fun of your child's clothes or looks. Or your child may be afraid of failing. After determining the cause, you can pray about it together and work toward a solution.*

Q: WHY DO KIDS ALWAYS WANT TO DRESS ACCORDING TO DIFFERENT FADS?

53

A: They want to fit in, to look like everyone else. Advertisers spend tons of money to make it seem as if everyone should wear certain clothes. Or a famous person might wear an outfit that looks good, and everyone starts buying a similar outfit. That's how fads get started. Soon it seems as though everyone is wearing the same styles and colors. But fads don't last very long. You don't have to dress in every new fad. Many clothing styles are classic and always seem to be in style. You can ask your parents to help you choose the right clothes to wear.

KEY VERSE: *Everything is so weary and tiresome! No matter how much we see, we are never satisfied. No matter how much we hear, we are not content. (Ecclesiastes 1:8)*

RELATED VERSES: *1 Corinthians 7:31; 1 John 2:16-17*

RELATED QUESTION: *Why do kids always follow the newest fad?*

NOTE TO PARENTS: *Let your children know that it's all right to wear the latest styles as long as they aren't too extreme. However, you'll want to point out that kids can be stylish without being faddish. Explain that fashion fads usually look pretty silly a few years later. To prove this point, find some pictures of fads from twenty years ago, or show photos of yourself as a kid.*

Q: WHY DOES EVERYBODY WANT TO DO THINGS THAT OTHER PEOPLE DO?

54

A: Because they feel pressured. They want to fit in, be liked, and not be too different. They may be afraid that kids will make fun of them if they don't do what everyone else is doing. Sometimes we assume that a movie, TV show, or product is good because it's popular. We may think, *If so many people do that, it must be fun.* Or, *If so many people have seen that movie, it must be good.* That's OK as long as what's popular is pleasing to God. But no one has to feel pressured to do things that are wrong.

KEY VERSE: *I didn't want to do anything without your consent. And I didn't want you to help because you were forced to do it but because you wanted to. (Philemon 1:14)*

RELATED VERSES: *Matthew 5:19; 1 Corinthians 9:20*

RELATED QUESTION: *What if someone says, "You won't be my friend anymore if you don't do that"? Should you do it?*

NOTE TO PARENTS: *This is a good time in your children's lives to teach them the importance of knowing the difference between right and wrong, having an opinion, and acting on what you believe. Peer pressure will increase dramatically as children get older.*

Q: WHAT SHOULD I DO IF OTHER KIDS LAUGH AT ME FOR GOING TO CHURCH?

55

A: You can ignore their laughter. If you get the chance, you can quietly explain that you go to church because you love God and because you enjoy church and want to be with your family and friends there. Someone who laughs at you for going to church may not know what church is, may have never been to church, and probably doesn't know what it means to love God and his Son, Jesus. That's someone for whom you can pray. You can even invite that person to go to church with you sometime, especially when your church has a fun night or other social activity.

KEY VERSE: *God blesses you who are hated and excluded and mocked and cursed because you are identified with me, the Son of Man. (Luke 6:22)*

RELATED VERSE: *Matthew 5:44*

NOTE TO PARENTS: *Most children don't understand the differences among the various religions and denominations. It's important for them to learn how to accept children from all cultures and backgrounds. They also need to understand, however, that they can't accept all beliefs. Help your children learn what is unique about the Christian faith and about your particular denomination so they will know how to explain what they believe.*

Q: WHY DO YOU HAVE TO BE GOOD AND OBEY IN SCHOOL?

A: School leaders and teachers have rules for how students should act in school so that the school will be safe and students will be able to learn. Just think of the confusion if all the kids did whatever they wanted whenever they wanted. No one would learn anything, except how to be rowdy. In class, for example, if everyone talked at the same time, no one would hear the teacher. And if kids were allowed to run, push, and shove in the hall, people would get hurt.

KEY VERSE: *Oh, why didn't I listen to my teachers? Why didn't I pay attention to those who gave me instruction? (Proverbs 5:13)*

RELATED VERSES: *Romans 13:2; Colossians 2:6*

RELATED QUESTION: *Why do you have to obey other adults besides your parents?*

NOTE TO PARENTS: *Sometimes children can become overwhelmed by all the rules in school. They may even fear that they might break some rules by accident. Help them understand that the rules make sense and that most rules are easy to obey. Help your children understand the long-term benefits of applying themselves in school and doing well. Point out that obeying school leaders is one of the ways that we obey God, who has given us these leaders.*

Q: WHY ARE SOME KIDS SO BIG AND OTHER KIDS SO SMALL?

57

A: People come in all different shapes and sizes. Just look at adults. Some professional football players weigh over three hundred pounds, and some professional basketball players are well over seven feet tall! Most people, however, are much lighter and shorter than that. Kids come in different shapes and sizes too. They also grow at different rates. A girl might grow quickly and seem very tall compared to other kids. But in a few years other kids will begin growing and pass her in height. It can be frustrating to be very small or very tall right now, but eventually these things average out. Be patient. Size won't matter so much in the future when everyone has finished growing.

KEY VERSE: *The Lord said to Samuel, "Don't judge by his appearance or height, for I have rejected him. The Lord doesn't make decisions the way you do! People judge by outward appearance, but the Lord looks at a person's thoughts and intentions." (1 Samuel 16:7)*

RELATED VERSES: *Psalm 139:14-16*

NOTE TO PARENTS: *Tell stories about when you were growing up and when you experienced your growth spurt.*

Q: WHAT IF I DON'T LIKE THE MUSIC THAT EVERYONE ELSE LISTENS TO?

58

A: You don't have to enjoy certain music just because others do. It's like with food. What if everyone else liked french fries, but fries made you sick to your stomach? Would you eat french fries? You wouldn't have to. In the same way, you will develop your own taste in music. It may be the same as others, but it doesn't have to be. Of course you should respect others' tastes too. Don't yell at them to "turn off that stupid music" just because you don't like it. Pay attention to the words, though. If you know they aren't pleasing to God, let your friends know you have no interest in listening.

KEY VERSES: *"Just as the mouth tastes good food, the ear tests the words it hears." So let us discern for ourselves what is right; let us learn together what is good. (Job 34:3-4)*

RELATED VERSES: *Romans 14:1-10*

NOTE TO PARENTS: *The fact is, at about nine or ten years of age, kids begin listening to the music styles that their peers seem to like. Beware of criticizing this music just because you don't appreciate it. Your children may interpret your criticisms as a put-down of their friends, not the music. On the other hand, be sure to point out specific problems you have with certain songs and stations (suggestive lyrics, depraved performers, dirty-talking DJs, and so on) and recommend alternatives. This is the ideal time to help your children learn to appreciate a wide variety of music. And remember that you probably can find a Christian artist for almost every music style.*

Q: I FEEL SO STUPID IN SOME SUBJECTS. WHAT CAN I DO?

59

A: Some subjects are difficult to understand at first—not everyone gets everything right away. God made each person different, each with special gifts. It's normal that some subjects will be easier for you than others. But you can still conquer the ones that seem very difficult. In those classes, you can ask the teacher for help. Most teachers encourage their students to ask questions and to ask for help when they need it. Your parents will also be happy to help you. Subjects that are difficult will help you learn to think and to figure things out.

KEY VERSE: *If you need wisdom—if you want to know what God wants you to do—ask him, and he will gladly tell you. (James 1:5)*

RELATED VERSES: *Proverbs 2:1-2; 22:17; 2 Timothy 2:15*

NOTE TO PARENTS: *Keep in mind that just because kids feel a subject is difficult doesn't mean they lack ability in that subject. Help your children understand that learning difficult material takes work. Do not use words such as stupid or dumb—never hint that your children don't have the mental capability to understand difficult subjects. Instead, challenge your children to do their best. Then give whatever help you're able to offer, find a tutor if needed, and look for ways to affirm your children's work.*

Q: WHY DO SOME KIDS SWEAR?

IF YOU WANT TO BE COOL
WITH AN "ATTITUDE,"
YOU CAN STILL BE COOL
WITHOUT BEING RUDE.
I'LL TELL YOU A SECRET,
I'LL GIVE YOU A TIP—
KEEP YOUR LANGUAGE CLEAN
TO BE REAL HIP.

Reee-aaow yuuo eererer

60

A: Usually kids swear or curse because they are trying to act older or cool. Some kids live in homes where their parents swear a lot, so they hear the words every day. Or they may have seen movies or videos with a lot of swearing. That makes it easy for them to use swearwords when they talk too. Swearing is a very bad habit to get into. In a certain group at school, it may seem as though swearing will make you accepted. But often people think that those who swear a lot are crude and not very smart. Swearing is *not* cool!

KEY VERSE: *Don't use foul or abusive language. Let everything you say be good and helpful, so that your words will be an encouragement to those who hear them. (Ephesians 4:29)*

RELATED VERSE: *Ephesians 5:4*

NOTE TO PARENTS: *Talk with your kids about swearing and why it's bad. Often kids will repeat a word that they have heard without having a clue about its meaning. When that happens at your house, be careful not to overreact. Instead, explain why the word is bad and help your children understand which words are swearwords and which ones aren't. If you have used swearwords yourself, apologize to your children. Ask them to pray with you, asking God to help you stop saying those kinds of words.*

Q: WHAT SHOULD I SAY IF SOMEONE MAKES FUN OF THE BIBLE?

61

A: If a friend makes fun of the Bible, you can politely explain how you feel and ask that person to stop. Your friend may not know how special the Bible is to you. This might give you a good opportunity to explain that the Bible comes from God, who created the whole universe, and it's very important to you. You might be the first one to help this person understand that the message in the Bible is for everyone in the world. If your friend doesn't want to listen, it's best to let it pass and just pray for him or her.

KEY VERSES: *But even if you suffer for doing what is right, God will reward you for it. So don't be afraid and don't worry. Instead, you must worship Christ as Lord of your life. And if you are asked about your Christian hope, always be ready to explain it. (1 Peter 3:14-15)*

RELATED VERSES: *Proverbs 30:5; John 17:17; 2 Timothy 3:16*

NOTE TO PARENTS: *Talk with your family about the significance of the Scriptures. Be sure your children understand that no other book ever has been or ever will be inspired by God the way the Bible is. God shows us in his Word exactly who he is, how much he loves us, and how important it is for us to love him. This would be another ideal time to teach your children how to explain to others what they believe. See* Ready for Life *(Tyndale House Publishers) for devotions that will help you do this.*

BEING COOL

Dealing with the Desire to Be Popular

Q: HOW DOES SOMEONE BECOME POPULAR?

62

A: The best way to become popular is to be a positive, helpful, nice person—someone that people enjoy being around. If that's the kind of person you are, kids who get to know you will like you for who you are. Eventually, lots of people will get to know you and like you. Whatever you do, however, don't pretend to be someone you aren't just to be liked by others. Be the kind of person God wants you to be, whether you become popular or not. In other words, be like Jesus!

KEY VERSE: *Be kind to each other, tenderhearted, forgiving one another, just as God through Christ has forgiven you. (Ephesians 4:32)*

RELATED VERSES: *Proverbs 10:32; Ephesians 4:29*

RELATED QUESTIONS: *How do you make people like you? Should I do what my friends do to be popular?*

NOTE TO PARENTS: *Most groups of children develop a natural pecking order, with the most popular kids on top. Children are very aware of this order, and most would like to move up the order. Several factors determine this order—height, attractiveness, silliness, etc. Explain that it's nice to be liked, but a person doesn't have to be liked by everybody. Also, don't be afraid to give extra attention at home. This will go a long way in preventing your children from worrying about their position in any pecking order.*

63

A: Nothing is wrong with being popular if it's for the right reasons. Some kids are popular because they are kind and caring. Sometimes Christians are very unpopular, however, because they stand for what is right. They have to say things that people don't want to hear and do what is right even though just about everyone else is doing what is wrong. (The prophets in the Bible sure weren't very popular!) It's much more important to have God's approval than to be popular with people.

KEY VERSE: *Obviously, I'm not trying to be a people pleaser! No, I am trying to please God. If I were still trying to please people, I would not be Christ's servant. (Galatians 1:10)*

RELATED VERSES: *John 5:44; 12:42-43; Acts 5:29; Romans 2:13*

NOTE TO PARENTS: *If your children want to become more popular, don't be concerned—that's normal and all right. They may be trying to figure out what to do to gain popularity. As you give advice about how to act at school, help your kids be aware of God's love for them as well as yours. Being assured of this love will help your children want to please God and please you, which will help fulfill their need to be popular.*

Q: DO YOU HAVE TO WEAR MAKEUP OR DRESS COOL TO MAKE PEOPLE LIKE YOU?

64

A: Some advertisements, television shows, magazines, and movies make it seem that way, but it's not true. Attention and popularity based on makeup and clothes don't last very long. People should like you for who you are. It's good to be neat and to *look* nice, but it's more important to *be* nice. People are drawn to others who are gentle and loving.

KEY VERSES: *Don't be concerned about the outward beauty that depends on fancy hairstyles, expensive jewelry, or beautiful clothes. You should be known for the beauty that comes from within, the unfading beauty of a gentle and quiet spirit, which is so precious to God. (1 Peter 3:3-4)*

RELATED VERSES: *Matthew 6:31-33; Luke 12:15; Philippians 4:11-12; 1 Timothy 6:8*

NOTE TO PARENTS: *Although most young children are not very fashion conscious, many of their parents are. Thus children of all ages can be found dressed like the magazine ads. This puts other kids under pressure to get new clothes all the time. Don't get caught in that trap. You can dress your children nicely and in style without spending a bundle on designer clothes. Let your children know that it's all right to wear the latest fashions (as long as they're not too extreme), but it's vital to be the right kind of person in those clothes. Character, not clothes, makes the person.*

Q: HOW DO YOU GET SOMEONE TO LIKE YOU IF YOU AREN'T AS POPULAR AS EVERYONE ELSE?

BE RIGHT WITH YOU MAX, MY MAN. JUST NEED TO ORDER A DOUBLE DE-CAF LATTE, AND TALK TO THE PRESIDENT OF MY FAN CLUB!

65

A: You can't force people to like you or talk them into it. And you shouldn't do whatever they say just so they will be your friends. When you live for Jesus and let the Holy Spirit control your actions, people will like you for who you are. So the idea is to help people get to know the real you. You can be liked, even if you're not voted Most Popular. Outgoing, likable people are often very popular, but you can be likable even if you're quiet. A few good friends who enjoy doing the same things can be just as much fun as a big group of the most popular kids. God made each person special and unique, so we should value all people (ourself included) no matter how popular they are or aren't.

KEY VERSES: *When the Holy Spirit controls our lives, he will produce this kind of fruit in us: love, joy, peace, patience, kindness, goodness, faithfulness, gentleness, and self-control. (Galatians 5:22-23)*

RELATED VERSES: *Luke 22:24-26*

NOTE TO PARENTS: *As kids grow up, they become acquainted with the pecking order in the various groups to which they belong. (See the note with question 66.) Look for groups—church groups, community choirs, and certain sport teams—where the other kids are more likely to accept your children for who they are. Usually the tone for a group is set by a caring adult.*

Q: WHY DO KIDS THINK SOMETHING IS COOL ONE DAY AND STUPID THE NEXT?

66

A: People change, so those kids may just have changed their minds. Think about times when you did the same thing. What was your favorite TV show last year? How about your favorite music group? Your favorites are probably different now. As kids grow up, they outgrow the things they liked a year or even a few months before. Also remember that fads change quickly. Something is "in" one day and "out" the next. That's a good reason for not getting too carried away trying to follow every fad that comes along.

KEY VERSE: *When I was a child, I spoke and thought and reasoned as a child does. But when I grew up, I put away childish things. (1 Corinthians 13:11)*

RELATED VERSE: *1 Peter 1:24*

NOTE TO PARENTS: *Children are susceptible to fads. Discuss the power of advertisements with your children—ads are the source of many fads. Have fun analyzing the advertisers' strategies and talking back to the TV together when one of those ads comes on. You can say, "Come on, I don't need that!" "Who are you trying to fool?" "No one will want one of those next month!"*

Q: WHY DO SOME KIDS ALL DRESS, TALK, AND ACT THE SAME?

67

A: People like to belong, to be accepted as part of a group. Many times kids will cluster into groups of friends, almost like a club. Then those kids will dress alike, talk alike, and act alike. Maybe they're afraid of being singled out or laughed at, or maybe they're all together because they just like the same things. It's all right to be part of a group, but be careful not to become a clique (a group that thinks it's too good for anyone else). And don't allow any group to convince you to dress, talk, and act in a way you don't want to or that you know is wrong. Be committed to what you believe, and be confident about your own tastes.

KEY VERSES: *If you love only those who love you, what good is that? Even corrupt tax collectors do that much. If you are kind only to your friends, how are you different from anyone else? Even pagans do that. (Matthew 5:46-47)*

RELATED VERSE: *1 John 2:15*

RELATED QUESTION: *If I want to join a group of kids, should I be like them?*

NOTE TO PARENTS: *Fitting in with peers can be a big deal to children. Try to accommodate your kids without going overboard. Let them know that it's all right to be like everyone else in a group as long as what they do doesn't keep them from pleasing God. Then encourage them to stay friends with others who aren't part of their group.*

Q: SHOULD I GET A COOL NICKNAME?

68

A: Nicknames are fun to have, especially if they make us sound good. But nicknames often come from others—the names describe how other people see us. It's not the same if we give them to ourselves. You don't need to have a good nickname to be a good person. If your friends give you a nickname that you like, however, let them know that it's OK for them to keep calling you by that name.

KEY VERSES: *These are the names of the twelve [Jesus] chose: Simon (he renamed him Peter), James and John (the sons of Zebedee, but Jesus nicknamed them "Sons of Thunder"). (Mark 3:16-17)*

RELATED VERSE: *Acts 4:36*

NOTE TO PARENTS: *Unfortunately, kids can pin cruel or demeaning nicknames on their peers, so don't give your children's peers any ammunition by using unusual nicknames with your children in public. If you have a pet name or nickname for your child held over from earlier years ("precious," "bunny," "babycakes," "champ," and so on), make sure it won't turn out to be used in a derogatory way outside your home.*

Q: DO YOU HAVE TO BE GOOD AT A SPORT TO BE POPULAR?

69

A: Good athletes are popular because people enjoy sports and like winners. But all athletes aren't well liked, and you don't have to be athletic to be popular. Don't try to be something you're not. If you're in a sport, do your best and play hard and fair—enjoy yourself instead of worrying about what others think. If you're not good at sports, most likely you enjoy other kinds of activities. Be yourself, and let popularity take care of itself.

KEY VERSE: *Physical exercise has some value, but spiritual exercise is much more important, for it promises a reward in both this life and the next. (1 Timothy 4:8)*

RELATED VERSE: *1 Corinthians 9:25*

RELATED QUESTION: *Why are heroes so popular?*

NOTE TO PARENTS: *Your children may suddenly become interested in sports or want to join a team because they want to be popular. Often kids will want to try a sport because other friends are playing. You may think that your children are doing it for the wrong reasons. That's all right. It may be a way to broaden their interests and skills. Sports will also help them develop social skills, such as teamwork.*

Q: IF SOMEONE ISN'T POPULAR, HOW COME OTHERS THINK LESS OF HIM OR HER AS A PERSON?

GET MUSCLE BUILDER'S AUTOGRAPH

ACME BODY PADDING

70

A: Popular kids aren't better than others just because of their popularity, especially if they are popular for the wrong reasons. Each person, including you, is a valuable creation of God. Looking down on others is never right, for the Bible teaches that all people are important to God and valuable in his sight. God wants us to treat everyone well and with respect. If you're wondering why more popular kids don't pay more attention to you, be careful that you aren't busy ignoring other kids who seem even less popular. Go out of your way to make others feel good and respected, no matter how popular they are.

KEY VERSES: *Then these righteous ones will reply, "Lord, when did we ever see you hungry and feed you? Or thirsty and give you something to drink? Or a stranger and show you hospitality? Or naked and give you clothing? When did we ever see you sick or in prison, and visit you?" And the King will tell them, "I assure you, when you did it to one of the least of these my brothers and sisters, you were doing it to me!" (Matthew 25:37-40)*

RELATED VERSES: *Psalm 100:3; 139:14; John 5:41; 1 Corinthians 4:3-4, 10-13; Ephesians 2:10*

NOTE TO PARENTS: *The real problem may be that your children believe that others think less of them. They may be experiencing rejection. When the social-life road at school becomes bumpy, the atmosphere at home becomes especially important. Spend one-on-one time with your children, for they may be the "brothers and sisters" for whom Jesus wants you to do things right now.*

Q: WHY DOES MY FRIEND ALWAYS WANT ME TO ASK PEOPLE WHAT THEY THINK ABOUT HER?

REMEMBER YOU ASKED ME WHAT FREDDIE THOUGHT OF YOU? WELL, I WENT AND GOT HIM. NOW YOU CAN ASK HIM YOURSELF.

71

A: Your friend may be unsure and afraid. She may think that no one likes her, and perhaps she is afraid to talk directly to people. Try not to get caught in a situation like this. Instead, assure your friend that *you* like her—*you* think she's special. If you would like to help her get to know more people, invite her to a group activity at your church. Or invite another friend or two over to your house when you invite her. If your friend wants you to ask boys whether or not they like her, it's better not to get involved.

KEY VERSE: *Encourage each other. Live in harmony and peace. Then the God of love and peace will be with you. (2 Corinthians 13:11)*

RELATED VERSES: *1 Samuel 20:3-17; 1 Thessalonians 5:14*

RELATED QUESTION: *Should you ask people what they think about you?*

NOTE TO PARENTS: *As kids get older, it's natural for them to begin feeling concerned with what others think about them. Help your children learn to affirm their friends, to make their friends feel good about themselves. Make your home a safe place where the friends feel welcomed and accepted.*

Q: SHOULD I HANG OUT WITH POPULAR PEOPLE TO BECOME POPULAR?

72

A: This may seem like the way to be popular, but that kind of popularity is pretty shallow and won't last very long. It's OK to be friends with the popular kids, but it's not OK to do whatever they say to be accepted by them. Instead, be the right kind of person, the kind that others will want to hang with. Be confident in the fact that God loves you. Remember that the Bible teaches us to think about the needs of others, not just our own. Spend some time and attention on kids who aren't very popular and help them feel good about themselves. You'll be amazed at how good *you* will feel when you make others feel good.

KEY VERSE: *Oh, that my actions would consistently reflect your principles! (Psalm 119:5)*

RELATED VERSES: *Proverbs 13:20; 1 John 3:18-19*

RELATED QUESTION: *If the popular kids won't let me hang out with them, should I ask why not?*

NOTE TO PARENTS: *Physical, mental, and social maturity varies greatly among children. In addition, some kids within a grade can be as much as eleven months older than the others. If your children are less mature, they may want to hang around with more mature kids to become more popular. But this probably is not a good idea. Get to know your children's friends so you can determine the kind of influence these friends have on your children. Encourage friendships with kids at similar stages of development by offering to have them over even before your children ask.*

MAKING THE GRADE

Relating to Teachers

Q: WHY IS IT THAT SOME TEACHERS ARE NICE TO OTHER KIDS BUT MEAN TO ME?

73

A: Most teachers try to be fair and treat all their students the same. But here are three situations that can make it seem otherwise:

1. It's easy to be nice to students who listen carefully, try to learn, do their assignments on time, and stay out of trouble. And it's natural to *not* be attracted to kids who seem to have bad attitudes.

2. God gave people different personalities. Thus, although we should love everyone, we get along better with some than others. This is also true with teachers. You'll find that you will get along OK with some teachers and great with others.

3. Some kids get nervous wondering how a teacher feels about them. Therefore, they misinterpret some of the teacher's words or actions as being negative toward them.

If you have problems with a certain teacher, pray about it; then do your best to cooperate and learn. That combination often works wonders.

KEY VERSES: *My child, never forget the things I have taught you. Store my commands in your heart. Then you will find favor with both God and people, and you will gain a good reputation. (Proverbs 3:1, 4)*

RELATED VERSE: *Luke 6:31*

RELATED QUESTIONS: *Why are some teachers tough? Why are some teachers mean but others nice?*

NOTE TO PARENTS: *If your child complains that a teacher is mean, don't judge the teacher. Instead, talk it through with your child to see if together you can figure out the situation. If that doesn't work, talk to the teacher and get the other side of the story.*

Q:

WHY DO SOME TEACHERS LET YOU GET AWAY WITH STUFF WHILE OTHERS GIVE YOU TROUBLE WHEN YOU DROP A PENCIL?

74

A: Some teachers are pretty relaxed, and others are more nervous and on edge. Some teachers have few rules in class, while others are more strict. One way is not better than the other. If your teacher is kind of nervous and strict, then be careful to act right and obey the rules. You can get along with any teacher if you try. Remember that even after you grow up, you'll always have to relate to different types of people. For example, you may have a boss who is strict. If you can get along with others, you'll have more opportunities to advance and succeed. If you can't, you may become frustrated and discouraged.

KEY VERSE: *A student is not greater than the teacher. A servant is not greater than the master. (Matthew 10:24)*

RELATED VERSE: *Romans 13:3*

RELATED QUESTION: *Why do some kids get all the attention and some just get into trouble?*

NOTE TO PARENTS: *Teachers who seem strict and keep their class under control are often more systematic and organized with their teaching methods. Kids who tend to be creative or people-oriented may complain about this type of teacher. But those types of students may benefit the most from this approach. Help your children understand that a strict teacher isn't necessarily mean—class discipline is more complicated than that.*

Q:

WHY DO TEACHERS MAKE IT EASY FOR SOME KIDS TO GET GOOD GRADES AND HARD FOR OTHERS?

WATER CONDENSATION MODEL (careful. hot.)

WATER MELTING MODEL (careful. cold)

75

A: It may seem as though teachers sometimes make it easier for some kids than others, but all teachers try to be fair. They really try to treat everyone the same. Also, most teachers are more concerned that their students try hard and do their best. They want kids to learn, not just get good grades. So they might push some students to work harder. Instead of worrying about others, make sure that *you* work hard and do *your* best.

KEY VERSE: *Brothers and sisters, we urge you to warn those who are lazy. Encourage those who are timid. Take tender care of those who are weak. Be patient with everyone. (1 Thessalonians 5:14)*

RELATED VERSE: *Ezekiel 33:20*

RELATED QUESTIONS: *Why do we have to have tests? Why do teachers have to grade tests? What's the point of a teacher drawing a happy face on your test?*

NOTE TO PARENTS: *Teachers may push kids who they believe are not working up to their potential. In other words, one student may work hard just to understand the material and pass the class, while another may be coasting to an A. The teacher may push the A student harder to challenge that child. Let your children know that the teacher may be tougher on them because they are able to learn even more than they have been learning.*

Q: WHY DO TEACHERS GIVE SO MUCH HOMEWORK?

76

A: Teachers give homework because they are trying to be *good* teachers and they want to help you learn. Doing assignments at home will remind you of what the teacher said in class and help you put it into practice. The school system was designed to include homework. It's not a punishment—homework is an important part of learning.

The best way to get the homework done is to start on it right away. Don't put off doing an assignment until the last minute. It's a good idea to do homework *first*, before watching TV, playing with friends, or talking on the phone. Even when you don't have assignments to do at home, you can review what you learned that day with your family.

KEY VERSE: *If you stop listening to instruction, my child, you have turned your back on knowledge. (Proverbs 19:27)*

RELATED VERSES: *Proverbs 17:16; 21:5; 2 Timothy 2:15*

RELATED QUESTIONS: *Why do we never get homework on Fridays? Why do we have to do homework?*

NOTE TO PARENTS: *Homework can be a blessing if it helps kids learn organizational skills and discipline. Help your children develop a daily schedule, and encourage them to do the work without your nagging. Too much homework may pile up on one night, especially if the schedule is already jammed. For example, one afternoon and evening schedule might include a music lesson, sports practice, and a Bible club meeting. When that happens, you will have to set priorities. Teachers, coaches, and church leaders will usually understand and work with you if you talk to them about your dilemma.*

Q: WHY WON'T THE TEACHER LET ME SIT NEXT TO MY FRIEND?

77

A: Your teacher probably knows that you won't learn very much if you're seated next to your friend. Sometimes when friends sit next to each other, they talk or pass notes instead of paying attention. The purpose of school is to learn, and teachers want their students to learn without distractions. You can still play with your friends at recess or sit with them at lunch.

If you do get an opportunity to sit next to a friend, pay attention and don't talk or goof around. When your teacher sees that you and your friend are paying attention and learning, then there won't be any reason to separate the two of you.

KEY VERSE: *Work brings profit, but mere talk leads to poverty! (Proverbs 14:23)*

RELATED VERSE: *Proverbs 23:12*

NOTE TO PARENTS: *Help your kids understand that it's good to have friends, and you are glad that they have friends at school, but learning comes first. Explain to your children the importance of obeying the rules and not distracting others, no matter whom they are sitting beside. Who knows, they might end up sitting next to a friend someday!*

Q: WHY DO WE HAVE TO RESPECT TEACHERS?

78

A: The Bible says that God expects his people to respect those in authority over them. That includes teachers. Also, for teachers to do their best, they need the respect of their students. If you respect your teachers, you'll be polite and kind to them, listen to them, and do what they say. Remember, the only one who benefits from your going to school and learning is you. If you don't cooperate, listen, and learn, you won't be hurting the teacher—you will be hurting yourself and your future.

KEY VERSE: *For the authorities do not frighten people who are doing right, but they frighten those who do wrong. So do what they say, and you will get along well. (Romans 13:3)*

RELATED VERSE: *Luke 6:40*

RELATED QUESTIONS: *Why don't some students respect teachers? If teachers want us to respect and obey them, they will first have to respect us as children. Right?*

NOTE TO PARENTS: *You may not always agree with your children's teachers, but let your kids know that you still respect these people. Teach your children that when you send them to school, you are extending your parental authority over them to their teachers and school administrators. So if they are disrespectful or disobedient to the school authorities, they are doing the same to you.*

Q: WHY ARE SOME CHILDREN SUSPENDED FROM SCHOOL?

79

A: The purpose of school is to provide a safe environment where students learn the things they need to know as they grow up. Children who break rules related to weapons, drugs, fighting, and so on, make it difficult for everyone else in the class to learn. Sometimes those kids have to be taken out of the classroom or even be suspended from school for everyone else's good. Hopefully their punishment will teach them not to threaten the safety of their classmates.

KEY VERSE: *Throw out the mocker, and fighting, quarrels, and insults will disappear. (Proverbs 22:10)*

RELATED VERSES: *Proverbs 19:25; 21:11*

NOTE TO PARENTS: *Just a few years ago, suspension was very rare in elementary schools. Recently, however, because of the violence among younger children, every threat is taken seriously, and children are being suspended for saying things like "I'll kill you" or "I'll get you." Help your children understand that a suspension is very serious. Kids who have been suspended from school may have done something more serious than the rest of the class realizes.*

Q: WHY DO KIDS OFTEN TAKE ADVANTAGE OF A SUBSTITUTE TEACHER?

80

A: Students think the substitute doesn't know them, the class procedures and rules, or what the kids have been studying. So some students think they can get away with things like being rude or not doing what the substitute says. If other kids ask you to join them in tricking the substitute, don't go along with them. Substitute teachers should be treated with respect, just the same as regular teachers. Besides, the substitute will probably leave a note for the regular teacher that tells how everyone acted in class!

KEY VERSE: *Give to everyone what you owe them . . . and give respect and honor to all to whom it is due. (Romans 13:7)*

RELATED VERSES: *1 Corinthians 16:10; 1 Peter 2:17*

RELATED QUESTION: *When our class gets a substitute teacher, why do we say that our teacher lets us out fifteen minutes early?*

NOTE TO PARENTS: *Even though giving a substitute teacher a hard time seems to be a time-honored tradition, we should let our children know that we expect them not to get involved.*

Q: WHY DON'T TEACHERS JUST GET TO THE POINT INSTEAD OF BLABBING ON AND ON ABOUT THE SUBJECT?

81

A: Some kids find it more difficult to learn certain subjects than other kids. Good teachers take time to teach *all* the students in a class, not just the ones who understand the material right away. Sometimes teachers explain other material that is also important, adding facts and reasons for what they are teaching. Listen and pay attention—you may learn something!

KEY VERSE: *[The Levites] read from the Book of the Law of God and clearly explained the meaning of what was being read, helping the people understand each passage. (Nehemiah 8:8)*

RELATED VERSES: *Joshua 8:34-35; Ecclesiastes 12:11; Philippians 3:1*

RELATED QUESTIONS: *Why do teachers explain things too much? Why can't teachers give you a sheet to tell you what to do? Why do teachers get mad at you for not understanding if they didn't explain very well?*

NOTE TO PARENTS: *In elementary school, teachers usually do not give long lectures. If your children ask this question, the problem may be that they do not feel challenged in class. Or it may be that one of your children has a learning disability or a different learning style and has difficulty understanding what is being taught. You may want to talk with the teacher about this. You could explain that you think your child might respond better to written instructions than to oral ones.*

Q: WHY DO MY FRIENDS GET FUN TEACHERS AND I GET MEAN ONES?

82

A: Let's face it, some teachers are more fun than others. Everyone is different, and it takes all kinds of teachers to teach all kinds of kids. But no one is trying to make sure that you don't get any fun teachers. Take a good attitude to class and give your teachers a chance. You may find that they are more fun than you thought. Also, remember the "grass is greener" syndrome—other kids may think that *you* have the fun teachers.

KEY VERSE: *Indeed, the Teacher taught the plain truth, and he did so in an interesting way. (Ecclesiastes 12:10)*

RELATED QUESTION: *Why don't teachers just let us play all day?*

NOTE TO PARENTS: *Encourage your children to have a good attitude toward their teachers. Teachers who seem mean may just be trying to establish their authority in the classroom at the beginning of the year. A few weeks later, those teachers may loosen up if the class is under control.*

Q: WHY DOESN'T THE TEACHER EVER CHOOSE MY PAPERS OR PICTURES TO PUT ON THE WALL?

83

A: Teachers usually choose very good papers to display in class. *Very good* may mean the highest score on a test or homework. *Very good* may be a beautiful picture or project. But *very good* can also mean showing great improvement. The teacher may want to recognize a student who has made great progress in the class. Do your best. It's an honor to have your work displayed, but don't worry about it. Just because your paper didn't go on the wall doesn't mean it's not good. Doing your best is more important than having a paper displayed.

KEY VERSE: *Be sure to do what you should, for then you will enjoy the personal satisfaction of having done your work well, and you won't need to compare yourself to anyone else. (Galatians 6:4)*

RELATED VERSE: *Romans 12:15*

NOTE TO PARENTS: *Look for ways to affirm your children's work. Display their tests, homework assignments, and artwork on your refrigerator or wall, complimenting them for doing their best.*

Q: WHY DO SOME TEACHERS HAVE RULES THAT DON'T EVEN MAKE SENSE?

84

A: Almost all rules have good reasons behind them. Sometimes, however, the reasons may not be obvious, so those rules may not make sense to you. It's all right to ask a teacher for the reasons, but be sure to ask nicely. It's important to have a good attitude in class. You should obey all rules whether you like them or not. If all the kids disobeyed the rules or just obeyed the rules they liked, no one would be able to learn anything.

KEY VERSE: *Help me understand the meaning of your commandments. (Psalm 119:27)*

RELATED VERSE: *Proverbs 6:23*

RELATED QUESTIONS: *Why aren't we allowed to chew gum in class? Why do we have recess for just half an hour instead of an hour?*

NOTE TO PARENTS: *Encourage and compliment your children for wanting to know the reasons behind rules. Let them know it's all right to ask questions like that. Be sure, however, that they really want answers and aren't just looking for an excuse to break a rule. When children understand the reason behind a rule and how people benefit from it, most of them usually have no problem following it.*

SUBJECT MATTERS

Succeeding in Class

Q: WHY DO WE HAVE TO STUDY SUBJECTS THAT WE MIGHT NOT NEED TO KNOW WHEN WE GROW UP?

85

A: People may think that the only reason to study a subject in school is to learn something that they might need in a future job. But that's wrong. Some classes teach information and skills that students can build on. Some classes teach students how to think. Most of what you learn in the early grades of school, such as reading and math, will help you in many areas of your life. Also, you never know when God will use you and what you have learned to help others. It will be exciting to see how God will someday use what you're learning now.

KEY VERSE: *Teach the wise, and they will be wiser. Teach the righteous, and they will learn more. (Proverbs 9:9)*

RELATED VERSES: *Proverbs 27:1; Daniel 1:4; 2 Timothy 3:17*

RELATED QUESTIONS: *Why do we have to study? If kids don't like subjects, why don't teachers make them more fun?*

NOTE TO PARENTS: *Encourage your children to try to do well in all their subjects. Help them understand that the things they learn now will prepare them for many things, not just for a future job. For example, they may need to know how to follow recipes, teach Sunday school, plant a garden, etc. Because no one knows the future, no one can predict which subjects will or won't be of value.*

Q: IF YOU HAVE ALREADY STUDIED SOMETHING, SUCH AS ADDITION, WHY DO YOU HAVE TO KEEP STUDYING IT?

86

A: To get really good at anything, a person has to practice. This can mean doing the same drills, playing the same scales, or reviewing the same material over and over. It's true in sports and music, and it's true in math and other subjects. Also, the simple problems will lead to more complicated ones. You won't be able to move on to the more difficult problems if you haven't mastered the easy ones.

KEY VERSES: *Then you will understand what is right, just, and fair, and you will know how to find the right course of action every time. For wisdom will enter your heart, and knowledge will fill you with joy. (Proverbs 2:9-10)*

RELATED VERSE: *Philippians 3:1*

RELATED QUESTION: *When my math is easy, why don't they give me hard math?*

NOTE TO PARENTS: *Textbooks and the curriculum of a school district are designed to review and reinforce previous learning. Usually the first part of each school year is spent reviewing facts and skills learned the year before. This may be boring for some children, but help yours to understand that it is necessary.*

Q: WHY DO SOME PEOPLE FIND A SUBJECT HARD, AND OTHERS FIND IT EASY?

87

A: Some people do better in math. Others do better in reading and writing. Still others do better because they work harder than most students. They listen in class, ask questions, and do their homework. Some people may learn a certain subject right away because God gave them the ability to do so. People are good at different things. Isn't that great?

KEY VERSE: *God gave [Daniel, Shadrach, Meshach, and Abednego] an unusual aptitude for learning the literature and science of the time. And God gave Daniel special ability in understanding the meanings of visions and dreams. (Daniel 1:17)*

RELATED VERSES: *Proverbs 14:6; James 1:5*

NOTE TO PARENTS: *Explain to your children that just about everyone has to work hard at some subjects. It may be because of something as simple as life experience. For example, a kid who has moved often and has traveled a lot may know geography better than those who have lived in the same place all their lives.*

Q: WHY IS IT SO HARD TO FIND THINGS IN MY DESK?

88

A: Probably because it's jammed with a lot of stuff. It's a good idea to go through your desk and take out all the notes, wrappers, old papers, stale food, broken pencils, and other extra materials that you don't need for your classes. Next, make sure that everything you do need is in there. Then organize everything; that is, put each item in a certain place so you know where it is and can find it when you need it. Try straightening out your desk at the beginning or end of each day. That will keep you from filling it with junk.

KEY VERSE: *Commit your work to the Lord, and then your plans will succeed. (Proverbs 16:3)*

NOTE TO PARENTS: *Make sure your children don't have such cluttered desks that they lose assignments, teacher notes, tests, permission forms, etc. If this is a problem for any of the kids in your family, talk with the teacher and design a course of action together.*

Q: HOW CAN I STOP DAYDREAMING AND PAY BETTER ATTENTION IN CLASS?

89

A: It's easy to let your mind wander and daydream in class, especially when you don't find the subject very interesting. One way to concentrate and stop daydreaming is to take notes about what the teacher is saying, maybe even write down questions that come to mind. If this doesn't work, ask your teacher for suggestions about what you can do. Teachers like it when their students *want* to learn, and they will be happy to help.

KEY VERSE: *Commit everything you do to the Lord. Trust him, and he will help you. (Psalm 37:5)*

RELATED VERSES: *Proverbs 2:1-4*

NOTE TO PARENTS: *Some children struggle with this. It's difficult for them to stop daydreaming once they've started. If you think this is a problem for any of your children, you may want to schedule a teacher conference. If your kids know that the teacher will ask them at least one question at the end of each class, they may be motivated to break the habit.*

Q: DO YOU NEED TO LEARN MATH ONLY IF YOU WANT TO BE A PILOT OR A CONSTRUCTION WORKER?

90

A: You'd be surprised how math is used in life. People in all kinds of jobs use math every day, not just pilots and construction workers. Engineers, writers, homemakers, musicians, doctors, managers, and even professional athletes use math. Go figure. Even if you just wanted to paint a room in your house, you'd use math to figure out how much paint to buy. Almost everything you learn now will help you understand the things you need to know later, whatever you end up doing.

KEY VERSE: *Intelligent people are always open to new ideas. In fact, they look for them. (Proverbs 18:15)*

RELATED VERSES: *Ecclesiastes 7:11-12*

NOTE TO PARENTS: *You can have fun with this by discussing a variety of occupations and showing how each one uses math. Explain how math is important on your job and in the rest of your life. For example, explain what you do when you balance your checkbook. (In addition, you can show how to divide the responsibilities at home by multiplying the factors involved in making your decisions!)*

Q: WHY DO WE HAVE TO LEARN GEOGRAPHY AND HISTORY?

91

A: Geography helps you learn about the world and gives you information about your own country as well as other countries and their citizens. People travel more than ever these days. One day you might be able to visit some of the countries that you have studied. Wouldn't *that* be exciting! Because of the Internet, TV, and other communication tools, people all over the world seem closer. History is an important subject too. It teaches lessons from the past that we need to learn so we won't repeat the same mistakes that people made before.

KEY VERSE: *All these events happened to them as examples for us. They were written down to warn us, who live at the time when this age is drawing to a close. (1 Corinthians 10:11)*

RELATED VERSES: *Deuteronomy 4:9; Psalm 106:7-8*

RELATED QUESTION: *What's the point of history?*

NOTE TO PARENTS: *One way to help your children see how these subjects are relevant is to talk about your ancestors, where they lived, and what was going on in the world in their time. Also, you might tell about a subject you didn't like when you were a kid, but which turned out to be important in your life.*

Q: WHY ARE GRADES SO IMPORTANT?

92

A: Tests and grades help teachers check to see what students have learned. Grades also help students and their parents see how well the kids are doing at school. Use your grades as a tool to help you see where you need to work harder. Remember that grades don't make a person better or worse than anyone else. More important than grades is whether you're doing your best and learning the material.

KEY VERSE: *Work hard so God can approve you. Be a good worker, one who does not need to be ashamed and who correctly explains the word of truth. (2 Timothy 2:15).*

RELATED QUESTIONS: *Do I need good grades? What's the difference between an A and a D? Shouldn't you always try your best, even in tough spots in life?*

NOTE TO PARENTS: *Some children need to be constantly held accountable for their grades, and they need encouragement to work harder. Other children get straight A's without even trying—these kids may need to be pushed to do extra work. Still other students may be obsessed with getting good grades and be devastated with a B. They might need encouragement to relax about the letter grade. Whatever categories your children fall into, make it clear to them that grades are a tool, not a goal.*

Q: WHY DO PEOPLE CHEAT?

93

A: People cheat because they're lazy. They don't want to work hard to complete an assignment or do well on a test. Cheating is wrong because it's lying, and God tells us not to lie. People cheat in many areas, not just school. Some cheat in games—trying to win without following the rules. Some cheat with money, and others cheat by not being honest with their friends. People who fall into a pattern of cheating find it hard to stop. Kids who cheat in school keep themselves from learning. Then they have to cheat again. After a while, people who cheat lose confidence in themselves and their ability to learn anything. Don't be a cheater—you will cheat yourself.

KEY VERSE: *Unless you are faithful in small matters, you won't be faithful in large ones. If you cheat even a little, you won't be honest with greater responsibilities. (Luke 16:10)*

RELATED VERSES: *Proverbs 11:1; 20:23*

RELATED QUESTIONS: *Can't you just look at one answer on a test? Why do some people cheat on tests and never get caught? Why can't I help my best friend with his math test?*

NOTE TO PARENTS: *It's easy for kids to get into the habit of cheating. If your children have been caught cheating, don't let them try to explain it away. And don't overlook an incident, rationalizing that it was a onetime occurrence. Also, don't think that one talk will solve the problem. Allow your children to experience punishment for cheating. Then return to the issue several times over the ensuing months until you are sure that they have learned their lesson and are determined to stop cheating.*

Q: HOW CAN I DO BETTER IN SPELLING?

94

A: The way to improve in any subject is to study and practice. You can become a better speller by reviewing the assigned words many times. Get someone to help you by testing you on those words. Your parents will be happy to help. Reading more will also help you improve your spelling because you will see words spelled correctly in the books. If you are writing with a computer and using spell-checker, stop and review the actual spelling when corrected. Ask your parents to look over your papers before you turn them in. If you keep working on this every time you write something, you will improve.

KEY VERSE: *Plans go wrong for lack of advice; many counselors bring success. (Proverbs 15:22)*

NOTE TO PARENTS: *Don't berate your children about the difficulties of spelling. Some children learn to spell more easily than others. Kids need to develop a working command of the language, but it should be fun for them. Take time to review spelling words with your children, and help them find a review method that works for them.*

Q: THE KIDS AROUND ME KEEP GETTING ME INTO TROUBLE. WHAT CAN I DO?

95

A: First, you can ignore the other kids. If you don't give them your attention, they probably will stop trying to get you to do what is wrong. If this doesn't work, ask the teacher to change your seat. To do your best in class, you need to be quiet and listen carefully to the teacher. Remember, no one can *make* you do something wrong or break the rules. Other kids can *pressure* you, but in the end *you* always make the decision. Decide that no matter what the kids around you do or how much they pressure you, you will do what is right. And you will do your best to focus on studying your lessons.

KEY VERSE: *Stay away from fools, for you won't find knowledge there. (Proverbs 14:7)*

RELATED VERSE: *Psalm 35:11*

NOTE TO PARENTS: *The first challenge is to see if the trouble is being started by the other kids or by your child. Don't be afraid to ask the teacher to move your child to a different seat, no matter who is initiating the trouble. Help your child understand that the they-made-me-do-it excuse isn't valid. Children need to learn that they are responsible for their actions and that their parents will hold them to that responsibility. This knowledge will motivate them to stand their ground.*

Q:

I WANT TO GET A'S, BUT MY FRIENDS SAY GETTING GOOD GRADES IS DUMB. WHAT SHOULD I DO?

96

A: It's always important to do what is right and to do your best no matter what others think or say. Some kids make fun of getting good grades because they don't want to work hard to get those grades. Others may think that it's not cool to seem smart. They're wrong. It's really cool to do well in school. Doing well now will lead to doing well in high school and college, which will lead to doing well in adult life. Kids who think that it's not cool to get good marks may think that they are somehow cheating the system, but they are only cheating themselves.

KEY VERSE: *It is senseless to pay tuition to educate a fool who has no heart for wisdom. (Proverbs 17:16)*

RELATED VERSES: *Proverbs 1:20-23; 9:12*

NOTE TO PARENTS: *This issue can be a problem for gifted students. Often, they get bad grades on purpose because they fear rejection from their peers. Parental support and friendship with other children who are interested in doing well in school can help to solve this problem. Sometimes peer groups will place a high value on doing poorly in school. This is why parental involvement is very important. Let your children know that you expect them to do their best, regardless of what others think or say. Of course your children don't have to broadcast or brag about their grades—encourage them not to do either of those things.*

Q: WHEN KIDS MISS A LOT OF SCHOOL, HOW DO THEY PASS?

97

A: Anyone who misses a lot of school will have a tough time catching up on the work. Kids who are ill or out of town on a trip sometimes get help from a tutor. When there is a good reason for missing school, teachers will give parents the assignments. Then the kids can do their work at home and try to keep up with the class. Parents can also help by teaching their children themselves.

KEY VERSE: *Learn to be wise, and develop good judgment. (Proverbs 4:5)*

NOTE TO PARENTS: *If this subject comes up, explain that just because kids are away from school doesn't mean that they aren't doing any schoolwork.*

Q: WHY DO WE HAVE TO STUDY COMPUTERS?

98

A: Computers are becoming a very important part of society, and they are getting easier and easier to use. Almost every kind of store and business uses computers—from grocery stores to car-repair shops. By using computers people can keep on learning more and more about almost everything there is to know. So studying computers will become more and more important. There is no doubt that computers will be part of everyone's adult life. People who know how to use computers will get good jobs and will be able to help others.

KEY VERSE: *Wise people treasure knowledge, but the babbling of a fool invites trouble. (Proverbs 10:14)*

RELATED VERSES: *Proverbs 15:14; 18:15*

RELATED QUESTIONS: *Why do people need to type? Why do we never play computer games? Why do we hardly ever get to use the computer, and then only for a little bit of time?*

NOTE TO PARENTS: *Most schools don't have enough computers for all kids to get enough practice on them. Your children might want more access, or you might want this for them. If you don't have a computer at home, let your child use one at the public library.*

SAVED BY THE BELL

Choosing Activities

Q: WHY DO SOME PEOPLE THINK THE INTERNET IS BAD?

99

A: The Internet has countless Web pages of all kinds, and it is expanding every day. The Internet can be a wonderful tool for finding facts and learning more about everything. Unfortunately, not all the information on the Internet is good. Some people tell lies on the Internet, and some Web sites have terrible pictures. When people read about these bad things, some of them think that the Internet is all bad. It's a tool, however, like a knife. Knives have many good uses, such as cutting and carving. But they can also be used for evil. The same can be said about television. It can be entertaining and provide helpful information, but it can also promote bad values and actions. Like all tools, the Internet can be used for good or evil. Make sure that you use it for good.

KEY VERSE: *Whatever you eat or drink or whatever you do, you must do all for the glory of God. (1 Corinthians 10:31)*

NOTE TO PARENTS: *Help your children know that the Internet can provide good adventures and dangerous ones. If you have a computer at home with Internet access, be sure to monitor your children's use of it, just as you do with television.*

Q: WHY DON'T I HAVE ENOUGH TIME TO PLAY?

100

A: Schedules get packed with activities, lessons, sports, and schoolwork. Sometimes it seems as if there's no time to play. If this is a problem for you, talk with your parents about it. After you have done your homework and activities, there should be some time to play. If your schedule is too full, you and your family can talk about the possibility of eliminating some activities.

KEY VERSE: *There is a time for everything, a season for every activity under heaven. (Ecclesiastes 3:1)*

NOTE TO PARENTS: *These days, kids are busier than ever. When teachers give too much homework, coaches call too many practices, and parents want their children involved in too many activities, time for play may get squeezed out. But play is an important creative outlet for children and a good way for them to reduce their stress. Be careful not to make your children's schedules too full. And remember that play is important for adults too—try to schedule time each week to relax and play as a family.*

Q: WHY DON'T WE HAVE GYM CLASS EVERY DAY?

101

A: Each school has its own schedule. The schedule depends on many factors: the number of students, the classes that students are required to take, the number of teachers, the rooms available, etc. It would be fun to have gym every day, but that might not be possible in your school. After school or on weekends you may want to be part of a sports team, take swimming lessons, or do something else you enjoy. You can do these things with friends or family.

KEY VERSE: *Physical exercise has some value, but spiritual exercise is much more important, for it promises a reward in both this life and the next. (1 Timothy 4:8)*

NOTE TO PARENTS: *This question may come from the fact that kids are full of energy and need a physical outlet. Organized sports and playing with friends can meet that need.*

Q: WHEN YOU ARE HOME DURING THE SUMMER AND NOBODY IS AROUND, WHAT CAN YOU DO TO HAVE SOME FUN?

102

A: Use your imagination. You could plant a garden, collect rocks or insects, take pictures, or check out the neighborhood to find some new friends. You could go to the library to read magazines and books or use the computers. You could organize a garage sale. You could ask your parents how you might help around the house. Perhaps these suggestions will help you think of other fun ways to keep busy during the summer.

KEY VERSE: *So I recommend having fun, because there is nothing better for people to do in this world than to eat, drink, and enjoy life. That way they will experience some happiness along with all the hard work God gives them. (Ecclesiastes 8:15)*

RELATED QUESTION: *What are some good things to do when you're not in school?*

NOTE TO PARENTS: *When kids seem bored, some parents merely tell them to find something to do and may say something like "Only boring people get bored." It's better to make specific suggestions and to offer help in finding something fun to do around the house. Help your children think of ideas themselves, by asking them questions and showing them how to go through a mental list of options.*

Q: MY PARENTS WANT ME TO PLAY SOCCER, BUT I HATE IT. WHAT SHOULD I DO?

103

A: Your parents probably have a good reason for wanting you to play soccer. They may want you to learn teamwork and good sportsmanship and to stay in good physical condition. So give the sport a chance. If you still don't like soccer after playing for a while, talk it over with your parents. Be respectful and explain how you feel. Suggest other ways to have the same kind of experience—like playing another sport or being in a club that you would enjoy more. It's good to learn a wide variety of skills. Soccer or something else you are learning may not be your favorite, but if you try hard anyway and see it through to the end of the season, you will learn lessons and gain another skill that you may use in the future. Your parents are more likely to grant your request for a change if they know you gave it 100 percent.

KEY VERSES: *Children, obey your parents because you belong to the Lord, for this is the right thing to do. "Honor your father and mother." This is the first of the Ten Commandments that ends with a promise. And this is the promise: If you honor your father and mother, "you will live a long life, full of blessing." (Ephesians 6:1-3)*

RELATED QUESTIONS: *Can I be involved in both baseball and soccer? What's a good sport to be involved in?*

NOTE TO PARENTS: *It's not easy to know when to push kids into something and when to let them make the choice. Try thinking of several options that will meet your learning objectives for your children and then let them choose. Don't give in the first time that your kids complain about an activity, but also avoid pushing them into something that they dislike intensely. Remember, you want to find ways to meet your children's needs, not yours.*

Q: I LIKE PLAYING THE PIANO, BUT I HATE PRACTICING. SHOULD I QUIT?

104

A: Getting good at anything takes practice. Practicing usually isn't fun, but it is necessary. Keep practicing—don't quit. When you get good enough to play music that you enjoy, you'll really have fun playing the piano. This works the same way in other areas of life. You've probably heard that practice makes perfect. This means that the more you practice, the better you will get.

KEY VERSE: *So don't get tired of doing what is good. Don't get discouraged and give up, for we will reap a harvest of blessing at the appropriate time. (Galatians 6:9)*

RELATED VERSES: *Psalm 119:34; 1 Corinthians 9:25*

NOTE TO PARENTS: *If your children like the piano but don't want to practice, this will give you the opportunity to teach personal discipline. If your kids hate the instrument, recitals, and practicing, however, you may need to find another way to expose them to music. They might prefer playing another instrument, or they may enjoy simply listening to CDs and attending concerts.*

Q: WHY DO MY PARENTS WANT ME TO BE INVOLVED IN SO MANY THINGS?

105

A: Your parents love you and want the best for you. They want you to have many experiences that will help you grow and be a more informed person. Because they don't know what you are going to be good at or what you're going to be interested in when you are older, they want you to try a lot of different activities now. You can learn a lot through music lessons, church choir, sports, and other activities outside of school. Everything you learn will help you enjoy life more. Be thankful that your parents are trying to help you learn as much as you can.

KEY VERSES: *You children must always obey your parents, for this is what pleases the Lord. Fathers, don't aggravate your children. If you do, they will become discouraged and quit trying. (Colossians 3:20-21)*

RELATED VERSE: *Proverbs 23:22*

NOTE TO PARENTS: *Children who ask this question may be feeling overwhelmed with their schedule. Being involved in too many activities can be dangerous for children because of the stress it creates. Children need time to relax and play even more than adults do. You may want to evaluate the number of activities and the kinds of activities you are expecting them to take part in.*

Q:

WHY DOES MY COACH CARE SO MUCH ABOUT WINNING? IT'S NOT FUN ANYMORE.

106

A: Sometimes winning becomes too important to people. In our society being number one seems to be most important. Coaches and parents can get caught up in this pressure. It's good to win, but it's also important to have fun playing a sport. If winning seems to be more important to your team than having fun, talk to your parents. Then they can talk with the coach. If nothing changes, you may want to ask your parents what they think about helping you get on a different team.

KEY VERSE: *So I saw that there is nothing better for people than to be happy in their work. That is why they are here! No one will bring them back from death to enjoy life in the future. (Ecclesiastes 3:22)*

NOTE TO PARENTS: *The pressure of having to win at a young age usually is not good. If your children are competitive, this may not be a problem. But most children are more interested in playing than in winning. Exposure to a high-pressure coach may burn out your child's interest in that sport. Changing to a different team may be the best solution.*

Q: HOW CAN I GET BETTER AT ART?

107

A: If you have talent in art, you will get better at it in the same way you get better at anything else—by practice. To get better at art, you need to do a variety of art projects. Ask your parents if you can get some art supplies for your birthday or Christmas. Then find creative ways to use things your parents are throwing out, such as old magazines and cardboard boxes. Get some scrap paper and spend time drawing or designing. You might ask your Sunday school teacher to help you find an adult at church who is artistic and would be willing to give you lessons. You may also ask your parents if there are art classes in your community that you can take.

KEY VERSE: *To those who use well what they are given, even more will be given, and they will have an abundance. But from those who are unfaithful, even what little they have will be taken away. (Matthew 25:29)*

RELATED VERSE: *Ephesians 6:7*

NOTE TO PARENTS: *When a child shows strong interest in art or music, Mom and Dad should look for ways to build on that interest and develop that talent. Outside of school, park districts and other community groups often provide classes and seminars where children—even the very young ones—can participate and further develop their skills.*

Q: I WANT TO BE WITH MY FRIENDS. WHY DO WE HAVE TO GO TO CHURCH SO MUCH?

CHURCH SERVICE

Sunday School

Club Meeting

SPECIAL KIDS'
SERVICE
Hosted by Jason
Meet at the
WAVE POOL!!

A: Christians go to church to worship God, study the Bible, and be with other people who believe in Jesus. Church is a special place where you can learn more about God's love and how to please him. Churches also sponsor clubs and other children's activities. Remember, you can bring your friends to church. You can also make friends at church.

KEY VERSE: *I was glad when they said to me, "Let us go to the house of the Lord." (Psalm 122:1)*

RELATED VERSE: *Psalm 55:14*

NOTE TO PARENTS: *Be sensible about thinking and then insisting that you and your family are to be at the church every time the doors are open. You may have to miss some activities and programs for the sake of your family. On the other hand, don't give the impression that regular church attendance is optional. Make worship and Christian education a regular part of your family life. Also do whatever you can to make church attendance pleasant, such as allowing plenty of time to get ready beforehand.*